STRATEGIC PLANNING
FOR BLACK FOLK

UNLEASHING THE SECRET WEAPON TO SUCCESS

DR. DORIAN R. WILLIAMS, SR.

Copyright © 2019 Dr. Dorian R. Williams, Sr.

STRATEGIC PLANNING

All rights reserved. No part of this publication may be reproduced, distributed, or transmitted in any form or by any means, including photocopying, recording, or other electronic or mechanical methods, without the prior written permission of the publisher, except in the case of brief quotations embodied in critical reviews and certain other noncommercial uses permitted by copyright law. For permission requests, write to the publisher, addressed "Attention: Permissions Coordinator," at info@beyondpublishing.net

Quantity sales special discounts are available on quantity purchases by corporations, associations, and others. For details, contact the publisher at the address above.

Orders by U.S. trade bookstores and wholesalers. Email info@ BeyondPublishing.net

The Beyond Publishing Speakers Bureau can bring authors to your live event. For more information or to book an event contact the Beyond Publishing Speakers Bureau speak@BeyondPublishing.net

The Author can be reached directly at www.StrategyBrother.com

Manufactured and printed in the United States of America distributed globally by BeyondPublishing.net

New York | Los Angeles | London | Sydney

ISBN Softcover: 978-1-949873-72-6

Dedication

I dedicate this work to our children—and their children.

TABLE OF CONTENTS

Preface 07

Chapter 1 Introduction to Strategic Thinking........................09

Chapter 2 Why Write a Book for African Americans?............19

Chapter 3 Inequality versus Inequity.....................................25

Chapter 4 You is Smart, You is Kind, You is Important!......... 33

Chapter 5 Developing Your Core Values................................39

Chapter 6 Decision Making: The Three-Move Principle™..........47

Chapter 7 Identifying Strengths, Embracing Weaknesses........... 53

Chapter 8 How to Conduct a Personal SWOT Analysis..............61

Chapter 9 Turning Your Dream Into A Vision 71

Chapter 10 Gather the Facts and Get the Information............. 81

Chapter 11 Developing Your Success Map 99

Chapter 12 Warning: No Discipline—No Destiny................111

Chapter 13 How are You Doing? Evaluating Your Progress............119

Chapter 14 Checkmate! Now What? 129

Chapter 15 The Strategic Plan: Putting it All Together 137

Chapter 16 The Strategic Plan Format 141

Chapter 17 Closing Remarks—My Final Move 149

Appendix   It's Your Move—Answer Key 155

Endnotes.. 157

About the Author 161

"... you have to face the fact that the whole problem is really the blacks. The key is to devise a system that recognizes this while not appearing to." [i]

Richard M. Nixon

PREFACE

Strategic planning is like the game of chess. In chess, the number of moves, choices, and possibilities in a single game is simply baffling. From a mathematical point of view, chess has at *least* 10^{40} positions. According to Jonathan Schaeffer, a computer scientist at the University of Alberta, "The possible number of chess moves is so huge that no one will invest the effort to calculate the exact number."

Like chess, achieving and sustaining success in life requires an *all-in* mindset. This is because each move creates another set of infinite moves. Therefore, each move must be meticulously calculated. In this book, chess is used as the backdrop to help readers grasp the power of choice. In chess, it is difficult to win without comprehending the consequences, risks, and rewards of each choice. It is impossible to consistently win without fully understanding the capabilities and the limitations of each chess piece. Even though each piece is different, their mission is the same: capture the king. Ultimately, all chess pieces are not equal, but each piece is necessary to win.

Similarly, in life, *pieces* may not always seem equal in importance. But they are. And when each piece is not aligned with your overall vision, you seriously hinder your chances of achieving success. Each piece—every move, will either increase or decrease your probability of reaching your goal. Strategic thinkers know this and realize the explosive power of aligning their choices with their vision.

This book teaches you to think and plan strategically, to align every decision with your core values. You also will learn why we, as African Americans, must use strategic planning principles for every one of our moves. Life for "us" is not spades, dominoes, or checkers—it's chess. Inspired by W.E.B. Du Bois' must-read classic, *The Souls of Black Folk*, I felt called to ensure my first book was for me—for us. Unlike other strategic planning books, this work approaches strategic planning from an equity lens, and is written directly for African Americans.

As African Americans, we must become experts at vision casting—we must develop a set of personal core values, comprehend the necessity of goal setting, and develop and execute a personal strategic plan. In short, this book will help you navigate life like an expert chess player. You will also quickly realize strategic thinking is the secret weapon to success. It's time we unleash it.

As a bonus, this book will introduce a whole new generation of people to the game of chess. For others who already play, this book will unveil the uncanny similarities between chess and strategic planning. Additionally, I believe it's time we *Black Folk* realize our strategic brilliance, our already present ability to navigate life's complexities.

Speaking of *Black Folk*, the data and my own first-hand accounts drove me to write this book for people who look like me. However, this book will help everyone—all disenfranchised people who are trying to overcome white-collar systems of inequity and discrimination. I believe it will also empower our non-minority brothers and sisters (*white folk*) with the type of socio-economic awareness our country needs to help us take on the equity fight.

I invite you to march with us—stand with us. Join us as we take on the remnants of these antiquated and exclusive systems; systems designed to stifle an entire people's progress, all in the name of color. Think back to those photographs from the sixties, when both black and white folk were marching together for the civil rights of African Americans. We welcome you to the fight—we need you in this fight!

I'm not a chess grandmaster, and this book is not intended to make you one either. However, this book teaches you to think like one where it counts—in life! Lastly, chess is a game *we* need to play, a game *we* need to teach our children and their children, too. Studies have shown playing chess raises your IQ, helps prevent Alzheimer's disease, exercises both sides of the brain, increases creativity, improves memory, increases problem-solving skills, improves concentration, grows brain cells, and ultimately, teaches planning and foresight. Let's play!

INTRODUCTION TO STRATEGIC THINKING

Strategic thinking is a process that defines the manner in which people think about, assess, view, and create the future for themselves and others (Bradford, 2019)[ii]. In order to achieve and sustain greatness, you must be a strategic thinker. According to an article published in *Forbes Magazine* (2019), there are ten unmistakable signs of strategic thinkers[iii]. The ten behaviors below are adapted from *Forbes*'s list and reimagined as your new traits as a strategic thinker. After reading this book, these behaviors will become part of who you are and how you operate:

1. You will be prone to self-reflection—One of the hallmarks of strategic thinking is the ability to unpack an event after the fact, dissect it to understand it fully and then internalize that knowledge, so you can do better next time. It's not about beating yourself up for a previous mistake — it's about living in key moments a little longer than others, so you can understand the bigger picture and commit to improvement.

2. Duplication of effort will frustrate you—Duplication of effort is where two or more parties perform the same work, or some of the same tasks, and end up wasting time and resources. You will find yourself grinding your teeth about this kind of avoidable waste of effort.

3. You will ask more questions than most—A strategic thinker is already working ahead to understand context, get ahead of any problems that might arise down the road, and make sure everybody involved understands what needs to be done.

4. You will learn to easily compartmentalize distractions—Crunch time is what separates strategic thinkers from those who are merely pretending. It will be easy to compartmentalize your many responsibilities and push distractions aside to focus on what's immediately relevant or whatever is the highest priority. Others might shut down mentally or even start to panic at the thought of seeing multiple projects through to completion at once, or in quick succession—but not you.

5. You will be decisive when you need to be—There's a notable difference between being decisive and being rash. Strategic thinking requires the former. It takes a strategic thinker to gather the necessary information efficiently, keep a cool head, and refuse to allow the weight of the decision to paralyze them.

6. You will regularly set goals for yourself—Goals are about never settling for "good enough," nor is strategic thinking. Setting goals doesn't always come naturally to everybody. You have to be able to break down major goals into tasks, and you need to know *why* something is worth the time it takes to improve it. You will learn to delight in setting personal and professional goals for yourself; it means you have your eye on the future.

7. You will enjoy helping others do their best work—Executing any strategy requires us to surround ourselves with people who understand the culture and the mission, and who know how to rise above challenges to get the work done. But realistically, you know everyone falls short from time to time or needs a helping hand. Strategic thinkers are people who delight in helping others do their best work and reach their fullest potential.

8. You will welcome and react positively to feedback—The flip side of helping others do their best work, is accepting help from others.

It's easy to assume we know what's best or believe our work is unimpeachable. Keeping an open mind and a collaborative spirit means everybody can speak respectfully and plainly in the interest of realizing across-the-board improvements.

9. You will speak deliberately—Communication is of the utmost importance when it comes to realizing our goals. Strategic thinkers are those who impart information clearly and deliberately, preventing questions or second-guessing later on. Plus, having and executing a strategy requires us to be able to explain it to others and secure their emotional buy-in.

10. You will plan your career in months and years, not days—You will regularly imagine where you'll be standing, and who you'll be, in one year or even five years' time. You will think about what your job will have in store for you next week and begin doing the groundwork today. You will not just float along—you will paddle and steer.

Strategic thinking is an extremely effective and valuable tool; it is the secret weapon to success. I learned this after my first week in Basic Military Training as a member of the United States Air Force (USAF). After only one week, it became painfully apparent you better have a plan, follow the plan, and constantly revise the plan.

I also quickly learned that punishment for not doing one of these things might be push-ups in the rain, marching until your feet became numb, or having a complete stranger scream at you—just inches from your face.

> *"Strategic thinking is an extremely effective and valuable tool; it is the secret weapon to success."*

My transformation to strategic thinking only intensified when the USAF decided I was fit-to-fly. In order to fly in the Air Force, I had to graduate Survival Escape Resistance and Evasion School (SERE). There, I learned to make use of every tool available to me to survive the most harsh and cruel environments. For this training, I was left for dead in the woods (in arctic-like conditions); then starved, beaten, and physically tortured, among other "confidential" things. Yet, I did more than survive: my classmates and I learned to thrive. We even felt the harsher the environment, the easier it was for us to succeed.

I graduated SERE training with a really ridiculous thought, "I couldn't wait for things to get really hard!" Because I knew when things got hard, when quitting seemed inevitable, when life became physically, emotionally, and psychologically taxing, I would have the strategic advantage over my competitors.

This advantage was not born from eating ants, crickets, and worms. Nor did the advantage originate from the psychological torture we endured at the hands of the world's most highly skilled "beat-down" professionals. The advantage was my realization that I've been strategic my whole life—so have you. We don't thrive as African Americans in this country without at least *some* strategic planning skill. Unfortunately, some of us are not thriving; some are just surviving. Not any more!

> *"…in life, your opponent is not a person sitting across the chessboard from you; your opponent is a system."*

I'm boldly challenging you to do more than survive; I'm challenging you to thrive. I'm going to teach you to move through life like an expert chess player. You will know every move before you make it, and you will also know every move of your opponent. However, in life, your opponent is not a person sitting across the chessboard from you; your opponent is a *system*. It's a system full of unwritten rules intended to stop you from becoming great. I'm inviting you to look the system in the face and to beat it. Let's play!

Once I realized its effectiveness, strategic thinking became my way of life. For me, everything became intentional and thought-out. As a result of my early grasp on strategic thinking, success became commonplace. I can even dare to say achieving success became easy. The more I applied these fundamentals in my life, the more success I achieved. My family and I followed the same process time and time again:

1. Set a goal.
2. Create a plan.
3. Follow the plan.
4. Measure progress.
5. Revise the plan as needed.
6. Achieve the goal.

Throughout my life, people are always interested to know how I went from being a depressed and sexually abused black kid, raised by a brave, but physically abused mother and drug-dealing stepfather, to earning three master's degrees and a doctorate's degree by the age of thirty-three.

These same people also want to know how I received a direct commission as the USAF's first African-American man to become an aerospace physiologist when I flunked out of college, blew a full athletic scholarship, smoked too much weed and drank too much. To me, there are four simple answers:

1. I released the guilt of my past, current, and future failures to my Lord and Savior Yeshua HaMashiach (Jesus Christ).
2. I thought about who I was, versus who I wanted to be.
3. I thought about where I was, versus where I wanted to go.
4. I had the audacity to do something about it!

Hilariously, people are really offended when I give them these answers. It's almost as if they are let down or disappointed in some way. Yet, it's true. One day, I just sat down, and wrote it all out. I began to think strategically about my life. Just like the Air Force taught me to think strategically about surviving a plane crash into enemy territory.

You see, strategic thinking results in strategic planning. And strategic planning produces strategic results. Trust me when I tell you, this is the one skill that current trailblazers and trendsetters hope you never acquire. I dare you to become a strategic thinker!

It's Your Move
(Answer Key is in the Appendix)

1. According to Bradford, "Strategic thinking is a process that defines the manner in which people _____, _____, _____, and _____ the future for themselves and others.

2. In this chapter, ten behaviors (see below) were identified that will become part of who you are and how you operate. For you, which two of the ten will be the easiest to exhibit? And why?

   _____
   _____
   _____
   _____

3. For you, which two of the ten behaviors will take the most work? Why?

   _____
   _____
   _____
   _____

- ⇒ You will be prone to self-reflection.
- ⇒ Duplication of effort will frustrate you.
- ⇒ You will ask more questions than most.
- ⇒ You will learn to easily compartmentalize distractions.
- ⇒ You will be decisive when you need to be.
- ⇒ You will regularly set goals for yourself.
- ⇒ You will enjoy helping others do their best work.
- ⇒ You will welcome and react positively to feedback.
- ⇒ You will speak deliberately.
- ⇒ You will plan your career in months and years, not days.

4. In this chapter you were introduced to six strategic planning fundamentals. List them here:

   1. _____   4. _____

   2. _____   5. _____

   3. _____   6. _____

Let's Play: The Chess Board

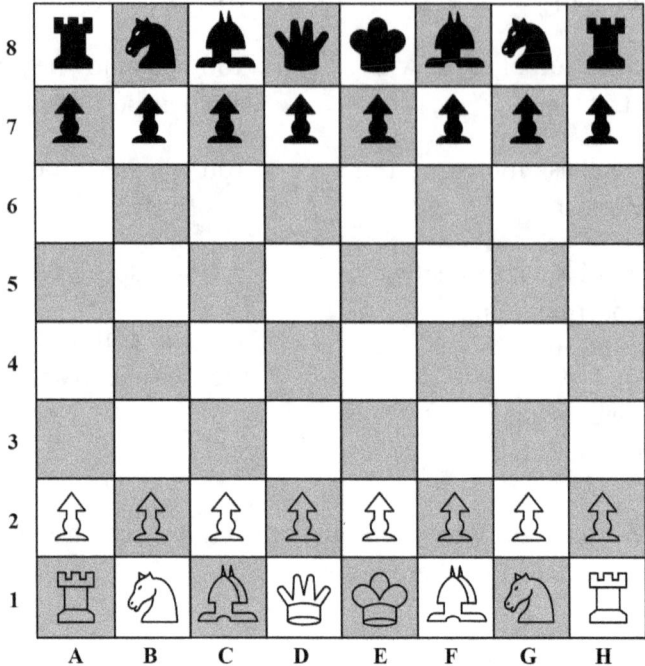

The chessboard is made up of 64 squares in contrasting colors and is divided by eight horizontal ranks (from numbers 1-8) and eight vertical files (from letters a-h), so that each of the 64 squares on the board can be identified. The board also has diagonals (from h1 to a8, for example). In the picture above, the E4 Square is a light-colored square intersecting the 4th rank and the e-file. This method of identifying squares is used when keeping score and is called Algebraic Notation.[iv] Each chess piece (except for the pawn) is identified by a letter:

- Rook = r
- Bishop = b
- Knight = n
- Queen = q
- King = k

The chess pieces or the chessmen are the king, queen, rook, bishop, knight, and pawn. The chess pieces are shown below:

King = K   Queen = Q

Rook = R   Bishop = B

Knight = N   Pawn

In the next "Let's Play" segment, we will discuss algebraic chess notation. Basically, this is just long way of saying how each move is named.

WHY WRITE A BOOK FOR AFRICAN AMERICANS?

Strategic thinking evens the playing field. Additionally, it helps you increase your capacity while intentionally becoming great at what you do. Strategic thinkers know achieving greatness is not an accident. Achieving greatness is a choice. Consider this statistic: "73 percent of successful companies have a formal mechanism to communicate their strategy", (Palladium Group Whitepaper, 2007).[v] This data is eye opening. However, a more critical point is intimated; successful companies have a strategy. What's your strategy? Are you communicating it? Remember, you better have a plan, you better follow the plan, and you better constantly revise the plan.

This book is not just a life-coaching manuscript on achieving success through strategic thinking. It is also narrative change; a toolbox for people of color—full of strategic thoughts, theories, and ideas that will influence your personal perspectives on achieving success. Ultimately, this book introduces success concepts to people who look like me. This is both the heartbeat and the inspiration of this work.

"My white friends will certainly ask, 'Why'd you write a book for African Americans and not everyone?'"

My white friends will certainly ask, "Why'd you write a book for African Americans and not everyone?" The reason is simple; the data says we are the ones who need this book. According to a study conducted by the Center for American progress (2019), "Wealth in this country is unequally distributed by race—and particularly between white and black households. African-American families have a fraction of the wealth of white families, leaving them more economically insecure and with far fewer opportunities for economic mobility."[vi]

As this report documents, "Even after considering positive factors, such as increased education levels, African Americans have less wealth than whites. Less wealth translates into fewer opportunities for upward mobility and is compounded by lower income levels and fewer chances to build wealth or pass accumulated wealth down to future generations." Or, as one Jewish Proverb states, "A wise man leaves an inheritance for his grandchildren."[vii] For African Americans, wisdom is not the problem. It is that we have little-to-no inheritance to pass down.

In 1619, the privateer vessel, The White Lion, brought twenty African slaves ashore in the British colony of Jamestown, Virginia. Among them were skilled craftsmen and farmers whose influence on the English is clear from the governor's order (in 1648) that crops be planted "on the advice of *our* Negroes."[viii]

Unfortunately, these *Negroes* did not have indentured servant papers, like most white servants did. As a result, "these new arrivals had no protected legal standing and could be easily exploited."[ix] Forty-two years later (in 1661), the first law recognizing the existence of slavery in Virginia was passed—slavery was now hereditary.

Expectantly, as landowners created laws to control the labor they needed, institutionalized slavery gradually evolved. The Slave Code was produced by the General Assembly in 1705—the rest is history.[x] This all but guaranteed an uphill battle for our children to receive an inheritance or any resemblance of accumulated generational wealth.

It should be no surprise the data supports that *we* need this book. Whether the mainstream media, or the hordes of "deniers" like it or not, much of our current condition is socio-economic, and the psychological result of the cruel, legal, and inhumane treatment of an entire race of people.

For two-hours one night, one of my good friends (a white) prominent and wealthy physician, lamented with me over these harsh truths. Believe it or not, that experience gave me hope. You see, what many people don't understand is most African Americans don't want a handout; we just want an honest cause-effect assessment—please.

As a result, I wrote a book for Black folk. The data was too compelling not to.

It's Your Move

1. True or False. Strategic thinkers know achieving greatness is not an accident.

2. True or False. African American families have a fraction of the wealth of white families, leaving them more economically insecure and with far fewer opportunities for economic mobility.

3. Research the following:

    o In your city, is wealth evenly distributed? Why/Why not?

    o In your city, what is the difference between the richest zip code and the poorest zip code? Why? How does it compare nationally?

- In your city, what is the percentage of minorities that work in your industry or the industry you want to enter? Why?

- In your city, is there a difference in post-secondary readiness and dropout rates between school districts or schools? Why? How?

- In your city, what is the unemployment rate? Why? How?

Let's Play— Chess Notation

Algebraic Chess Notation describes each move with the name of the pieces and the square to which it is moved. Each piece has its own letter abbreviation, except the pawn. If no piece is named, it's assumed to be a pawn move. Remember, the Knight is "N" not "K", which is King. In the figure below[xi] the move is e4. The name of this move is simply "e4", since the pawn's has no letter associated with it.

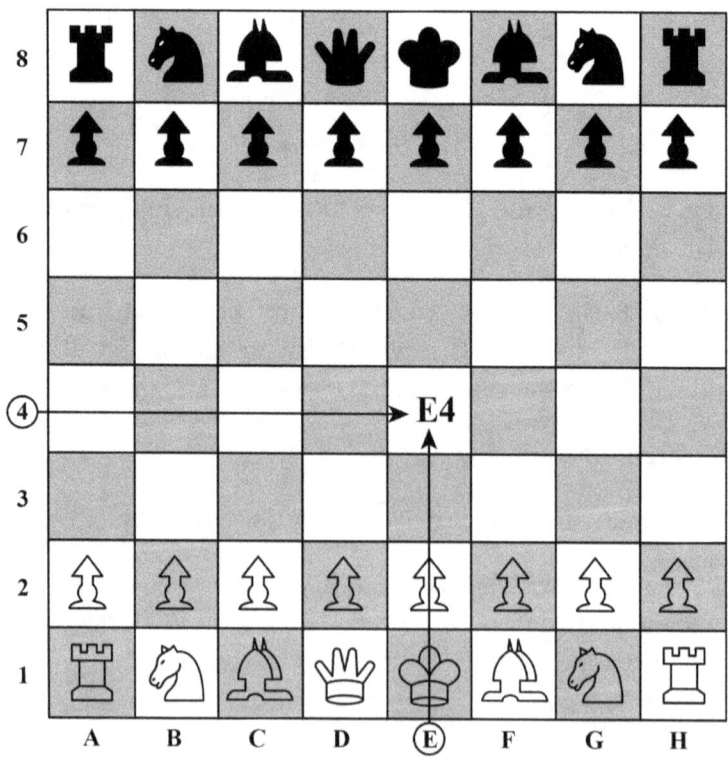

www.strategybrother.com

Black has made a pawn move, written as e5. White replied Nf3 (Knight to square f3).[xii]

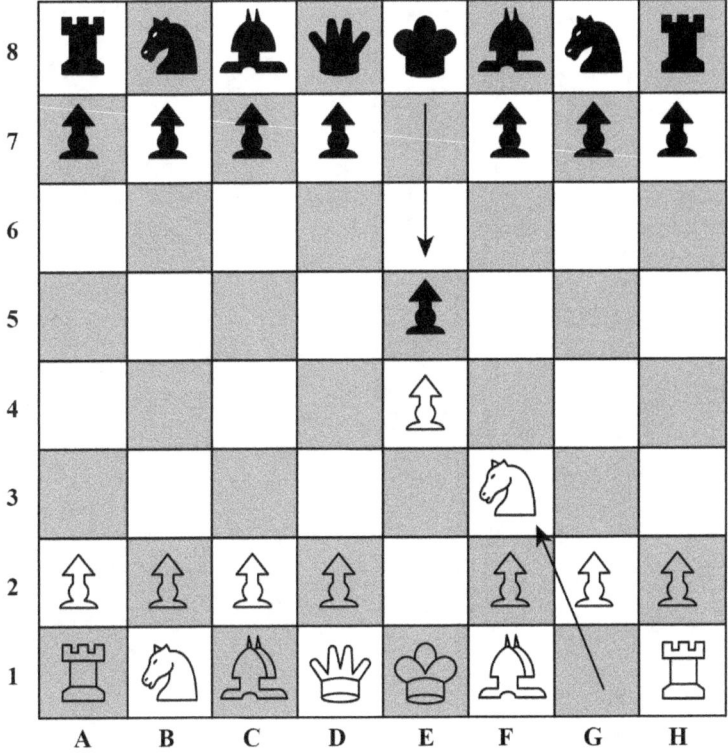

Over the next few "Let's Play" segments, we will discuss each chess piece and how they move.

CHAPTER THREE

INEQUITY VERSUS INEQUALITY

It's more difficult for us. Whether intentional or not, African Americans have been operating on systemically reduced opportunities when compared to our similarly qualified counterparts. In no way am I blaming our *honest* counterparts for this issue. I am however, blaming the current systems designed to encourage exclusivity and prevent equitable entry points. These entry point barriers affect the job market, access to quality education and to quality-affordable health care.

> *"It's more difficult for us."*

Like the chessboard itself, these *systems* are often designed in black and white and can only be navigated by those with intimate knowledge of the existing system. A casual knowledge of the board is not good enough; great chess players know the board dimensions, number of squares, etc. Ultimately, the advantage goes to the person with the most awareness and knowledge of the board.

Yes, knowledge of the board will empower you to expertly read the chessboard. But, consider this. What if this knowledge is only gained by reading a book on chess? And what if it was illegal for people with blue skin to learn to read? It would be virtually impossible for people with blue skin to win a game. Therefore, an inequity exists, because blue-

STRATEGIC PLANNING 25

skinned chess players do not have the same starting point as non-blue skinned players. This is inequity.

I have discovered that many get the term equality confused with equity. This confusion results in an attitude that African Americans now have equal rights and therefore, all is fair. This is simply not true. Equality only works if all parties have the same starting point or the same opportunities. The best way to contrast the two terms is to note that equality is about sameness, while equity is about fairness. Equity is the process; equality is an outcome. In other words, "equity is essential to achieve true equality."[xii] The Race Matters Institute says, "The route to achieving equity will not be accomplished through treating everyone equally. It will be achieved by treating everyone equitably, or justly according to their circumstances."[xiv] See the figure below for a great illustration on equity versus equality.

Equality = SAMENESS

Equality is about SAMENESS, it promotes fairness and justice by giving everyone the same thing.

BUT it can **only work IF everyone starts from the SAME place**, in this example equality only works if everyone is the same height.

Equity = FAIRNESS

EQUITY is about FAIRNESS, it's about making sure people get access to the same opportunities.

Sometimes our differences and/or history, can create barriers to participation, so we must **FIRST** ensure EQUITY before we can enjoy equality.

www.strategybrother.com

I did not fully understand inequity until I moved back home to San Antonio, Texas. While San Antonio is well known for the Alamo and the Riverwalk, there is something else that gets largely ignored. San Antonio leads the country in economic segregation. In San Antonio, your race and zip code are predictive indicators of your attainment of wealth, your quality of education, and even quality of care in your golden years. As of 2019, San Antonio, Texas overtook Detroit, Michigan as the most impoverished major metropolitan city in America.[xv] This is not just a social or an economic problem, it's far worse. It's systemic.

After a quick literature review, I shockingly discovered the San Antonio *system* was intentionally created to exclude minorities from what is commonly known as *the American Dream*. According to an article by the Rivard Report (2016), Christine Drennon, PhD, Texas geographer and associate professor of sociology and anthropology at Trinity University says "Historically, we created a racially, ethnically, and economically differentiated landscape...and then we applied a set of standards to the entire thing, regardless of geography, and with that, it had a lot of unanticipated consequences."[xvi]

Dr. Drennon is speaking of how San Antonio's urban development in the early 20th century forbade African Americans and Hispanics from living in upscale and wealthier neighborhoods. As a result, minorities were forced into poorly planned, under sourced, industrial areas, on the city's West and East Side. It didn't end there. Federal redlining laws reinforced this intentional segregation by literally "red lining" certain areas that were deemed "definitely declining" and "hazardous." Any areas or residents within these *red lines* had zero access to the city's economic growth. This all but ensured generational poverty for San Antonio minorities like my family and me.

Banks and lending institutions were also out of reach and could now legally justify denying East and Westside residents home or business loans. Below is a hand-colored map from the 1930s that shows redlining of San Antonio's near downtown area for real estate investment purposes. Remember, this was done intentionally—systemically. The map below is a historical *Redlined* map housed at the University of Texas at San Antonio in the digital collection.

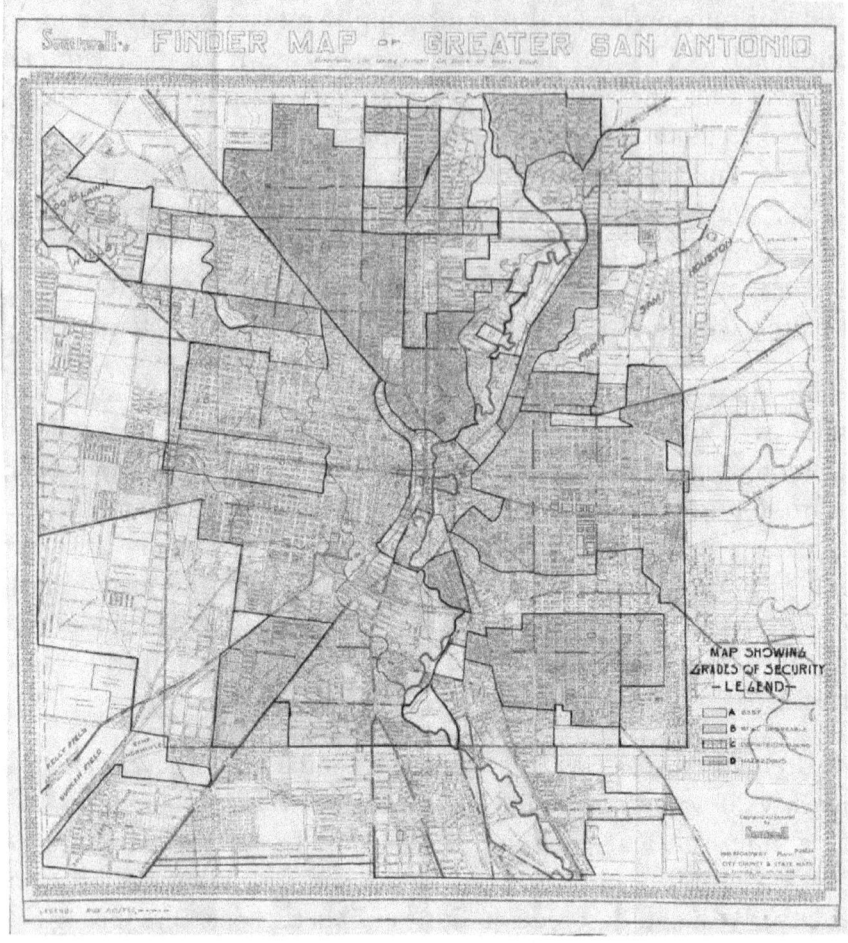

Dr. Drennon echoes this by stating, "We didn't do this because people liked to live with people they looked like – you know, we hear that all the time …We did this with policy. This was the United States policy that produced this very differentiated landscape of who looks like what and how much money is going in there."

The report further cites Dr. Drennon as saying, "We've created inequality. We created it through policy, we inhabited it, we took ownership of it, we live it, but then we try to treat the whole thing the same… and

"Except for Maryland and Kentucky— Southern states absolutely prohibited the education of slaves."

when stuff isn't equitable, we wonder: 'Well what's wrong with you?' We don't think about some of the legacies that are actually built into the system."

This truth has had a devastating impact on progression of minorities in my beloved city. And while this book is not an indictment on my town, it is the truth that fuels my passion. While travelling the world, I noticed these systems were interconnected. Like my people back in San Antonio, African Americans all over the country were also fighting a *system*.

The Fourteenth Amendment to the Constitution (1868) is another example of inequity. This amendment granted African Americans the rights of citizenship. However, this did not always translate into the ability to vote. Unfair rules, such as poll taxes, literacy tests, fraud and intimidation, all turned African Americans away from the polls.

In this case, yes, African Americans had an equal right to vote. However, if they could not pass a literacy test, they could not vote. Therefore, the Fourteenth Amendment was not equitable for African Americans in the south. It was not equitable, because it didn't consider the anti-literacy laws that forbade African Americans from learning to read or write. Except for Maryland and Kentucky—Southern states absolutely prohibited the education of slaves.

The same inequity was seen with poll taxes. Many companies intentionally refused to hire, and/or discriminated against African-Americans. As a result, the majority of those unemployed were African Americans. Expectantly, we were unable to pay the poll tax that accompanied voting. How is that fair and equitable? It is unbelievable that this went on for almost 150 years and was not addressed until the civil rights movement. Resultantly, the Voting Rights Act of 1965 abolished the literacy tests and poll taxes purposely designed to disenfranchise African-American voters.

In response to the many states that fought back to keep their poll taxes in place, Supreme Court Justice William Douglas was cited as stating, "Wealth, like race, creed, or color, is not germane to one's ability to participate intelligently in the electoral process. Lines drawn on the basis of wealth or property, like those of race, are traditionally disfavored. To introduce wealth or payment of a fee as a measure of a voter's qualifications is to introduce a capricious or irrelevant factor. The degree of the discrimination is irrelevant."

He concluded, "To repeat, wealth or fee paying has, in our view, no relation to voting qualifications; the right to vote is too precious, too fundamental to be so burdened or conditioned."[xvii] Thank you—*smh*.

Systems of inequity are the primary reason for minorities (blue-skinned people) to obtain high-level strategic planning skills. You need to recognize when a system is unfair, and then you must develop a strategy to defeat it. After you have defeated it, you should then create entry points for others to follow your lead—à la Harriet Tubman.

In my opinion, Mrs. Tubman wasn't helping slaves run *from* something, she was helping run *to* something. She figured out a way to be free, then shared the way with others. In other words, when you get *yours*, help somebody else get *theirs* too. **Note:** You can't claim to be progressive and responsible, yet succumb to the *crabs in a barrel* mindset. I digress.

As African Americans, we cannot be strategic thinkers if we are not willing to study and research the existing systems of inequity. In other words, in order to play the game, we must know the board. The most effective way to research a system is by asking "Why?" and then, by asking "How?"

"This is our fight, our 21st Century civil-rights movement."

Knowledge of existing systems of inequity will empower you as a strategic thinker, but comprehending these systems will show you where to start in your strategic planning process. Yes, a well-executed strategic plan will get you a seat at the *table*. However, after you are at the table, you must do more than just happily sit there; you must begin working to restructure the system to create equitable entry points for all. Not just for other African Americans, but for all of those who have been systemically engineered out of the success equation. I call this the "Tubman Tactic".

This is our fight, our 21st Century civil-rights movement. We have been handed the baton from those who have spent a lifetime ensuring people of color had *equal rights*. Now, we must walk into the 2.0. equity version of their work. Version 2.0. is less about marching and protests, and more about infiltration and strategy. We must strategically enter the system with the intent to revise it. Calling all the *Tubmans—where you at?*

It's Your Move

1. True/False. Systems of inequity are the primary reason for minorities to obtain high-level strategic planning skill.

2. Equality only works if all parties have the same _____ or the same opportunities.

3. True/False. Systems of inequity are the primary reason for minorities to obtain high-level strategic planning skills.

4. You need to recognize when a system is unfair, and then you must develop a _____ to defeat it. After you have defeated it, you should then create _____ _____ for others to follow your lead.

5. What made the Fourteenth Amendment not equitable?

6. From your research, did you find that your city had any inequity issues? What were they?

Let's Play: The Pawn

The pawn chess piece is often the most overlooked of all the chess pieces. The piece, itself, is very simple. On most chess sets, the pawn chess piece is the smallest piece on the board. Each player begins a chess game with eight pawns, standing in front of their other eight chess pieces. Pawns are both simple and complex in their movements. The pawn piece has the fewest options of any chess piece on the board in where it can move, and it can only move forward until it reaches the other side of the board. Here are a few things to know about how a pawn chess piece moves:

- Pawn chess pieces can only move directly forward one square, with two exceptions:
    - ⇒ Pawns can move directly forward two squares on their first move only.
    - ⇒ Pawns can move diagonally forward when capturing an opponent's chess piece.
- Once a pawn chess piece reaches the other side of the chess board, the player may "trade" the pawn in for any other chess piece if they choose, except another king.

Pawn Names and Terms—Not all pawns are created equal. Each pawn is named after the piece behind it. For example, the two outer pawns are called "Rook Pawns", while the pawns in front of the King and Queen at the start of a game are called "King Pawn" and "Queen Pawn" respectively. In addition, pawns on each side of the board are named. This is to help clarify which pawn is which, when referring to a Bishop Pawn, Knight Pawn, or Rook Pawn. The pawns on the Queen's side of the board are called Queen side pawns, and the pawns on the King's side of the board are called King side pawns. Your opponent's pawn directly across the board from your own pawn is called the "Counterpawn".[xviii]

CHAPTER FOUR

YOU IS SMART, YOU IS KIND, YOU IS IMPORTANT!

To become a strategic thinker, you must first know who you are. You must see yourself as a champion. A winner. An overcomer. You must become an expert at ignoring false portrayals of you by other people. This is especially true regarding mainstream and social media. You will never master the art of strategic thinking if you let other people think for you.

Strategic thinking begins and ends with creating and sustaining a positive identity of self. Regardless of what others say, you must ALWAYS believe, "You is smart, you is kind, you is important!" (Kathryn Stockett, *The Help*). This is not always easy, especially for African Americans. Words of affirmation and positive portrayals of African Americans are not always easy to find.

"You cannot know what you want to be when you grow up, if you don't know who you want to be when you grow up."

The gross lack of strategic thinkers, engaging mentors, and positive role models in the black community is astounding. You cannot know *what* you want to be when you grow up, if you don't know *who* you want to be when you grow up. Listen, if you are passionate about seeing people

STRATEGIC PLANNING

win, I implore you: please get some training and become a community mentor or life coach. Reading this book is a great start.

Growing up as a black male in the early eighties, I often suffered from the effects of subconscious identity crises. Who was I supposed to become? Was I supposed to be like one of the many sports figures who inundated my television set? I was certainly supposed to be like those larger-than-life sports icons that our fathers, uncles, and barbers worshipped. Right? Or maybe, I was supposed to pattern myself after the hordes of entertainers I heard on the radio?

> *"Black depictions on television have an effect on viewers of all ages and of all races."*
>
> *Punyanunt-Carter, 2008*

You see, during that time, most black boys dreamt we were a part of the Los Angeles Lakers. We could see ourselves taking passes from Magic Johnson, and then finishing the fast break with a rim-rocking slam-dunk over Larry Bird. Yeah, *showtime* baby, that was it! Or, was it? Sigh.

Others envisioned themselves as athletes, such as Walter Payton, Tony Dorsett, or the great Florence Griffith-Joyner (aka "Fol-Jo"). Some of us longed to be entertainers like Run D.M.C., Kurtis Blow, M.C. Lyte, New Edition, Salt-N-Pepa, or Big Daddy Kane. And who could forget Debbie Thomas! She was the first African-American female figure skater most of us ever saw on television. As a matter of fact, I'm sure the identity crisis was even more of an issue for young black girls. After all, they had two strikes against them, as there were even fewer success portraits for them to trace.

In no way am I blaming (solely) the media for our identity struggles. I am, however, pointing to the fact that very few black kids in my neighborhood had blueprints to compare what we saw on TV against real life. As a matter of fact, most of my friends were living fatherless existences, being raised by single mothers, or had broken and dysfunctional relationships with their families. To us, that was real life.

Research findings (Punyanunt-Carter, 2008)[xix] have consistently shown that "negative exposure to African-American portrayals in the media significantly influences the evaluations of African Americans in general. Black depictions on television have an effect on viewers of all ages and of all races."[xx]

Carter goes on to say, "Media portrayals of African Americans have been frequently crafted around stereotypical occupational roles, with negative personality characteristics, as low achievers, and with blatantly obvious stereotypes."[xxi]

When the absence of real-life experience exists, people believe that what is portrayed is real. This has resulted in decades of bias, stereotyping, profiling, and even worse: it has negatively affected the African-American community's belief in our own ability to achieve greatness.

So, here is the crux of the matter. We have given media too much power. You cannot become a strategic thinker when you spend more time engaged in social media, television or radio shows, etc., than executing your plan or living out your core values (more about your core values in chapter four). Your time is too valuable to give it away. Your perception of yourself is too critical to burn negative portrayals of yourself and your community into your psyche.

A new study suggests that people who watched more than three hours of TV per day (on average) over the next 25 years were more likely to perform poorly on certain cognitive tests, compared to people who watched little TV. It is not fully known why spending more time watching TV is linked to poor cognitive performance later in life. Behavioral expert and licensed mental health professional Ken Parker suggests it may be because "television viewing is not a cognitively engaging way to spend time."[xxii]

"...before we can learn to think strategically, we must first learn to unthink what we have been conditioned to believe about ourselves."

A Neilson report found that the average American watches more than 34 hours of television each week. There is nothing strategic about watching hours of television or being glued to an electronic device. Mainstream media is powerful—too powerful. One could even say it is the enemy of strategic thinking.

There is a reason most of my generation grew up thinking we wanted to be athletes or entertainers: it was what we saw. What you watch affects you. Immediately stop watching what you don't want to be. Anything (anyone) that can mentally, spiritually, or physically influence an entire culture must operate with great care and responsibility. Is mainstream media responsible? Hell no! Therefore, before we can learn to think strategically, we must first learn to *unthink* what we have been conditioned to believe about ourselves.

You are more than what you see on social media, music videos, and on the television. Do not let your perception of self be defined by a writer or music producer. Rather, seek out a real-life person to be your mentor. Hire an expert to help you develop a healthy definition of what success looks like for you. Remember, "You is smart, you is kind, you is important!"

It's Your Move

Write down all the shows you watched this week and how long they were (including commercials if it was live), including movies, YouTube videos, social media, video games, etc.

Take that number and divide it by seven. This is a rough estimate of how much daily time you spend in front of the screen or some device. Please write it as big as you can on the screen below.

The number on the screen above is how many hours you're losing each day to some form of media. After you finish this book, I challenge you to reallocate at least 1/3rd of this time to daily planning, executing, evaluating, and revising your strategic plan. Please, schedule yourself for this "personal development" time. If necessary, you may want to go to a coffee shop or bookstore during this time to ensure you are focused and not distracted. **Note:** This is a scheduled appointment, please do not miss it or be late.

Let's Play: The Rook

The straight piece—that's the easiest way to describe the rook chess piece. In traditional sets, the piece looks kind of like a castle tower and begins each chess game as the outside corner pieces. Each player has two rook pieces to begin. The rooks are the most simple-moving chess pieces on the board. Their movements are only straight, moving forward, backward, or side-to-side. At any point in the game, the piece can move in any direction that is straight ahead, behind, or to the side. Here are a few things to know about how the rook chess piece moves:

- The rook piece can move forward, backward, left or right at any time.

- The rook piece can move anywhere from one to seven squares in any direction, as long as it is not obstructed by any other piece.

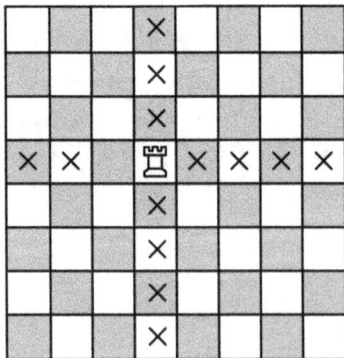

Castling—The rook piece is the only piece on the board that can participate in a "castling" move with the king piece. This is a move where the king piece and the rook piece work together, allowing the player to move two pieces at the same time. We'll discuss castling later.[xxiii]

CHAPTER FIVE

DEVELOPING YOUR CORE VALUES

For this work, core values are defined as the fundamental beliefs of a person or family. Your core values serve as a set of guiding principles that help you make aligned decisions or moves. Alignment is when all decisions, ideas, and actions agree with your overall mission and goals. The figure below illustrates how a decision can be out of alignment with your overall goals or you core values.

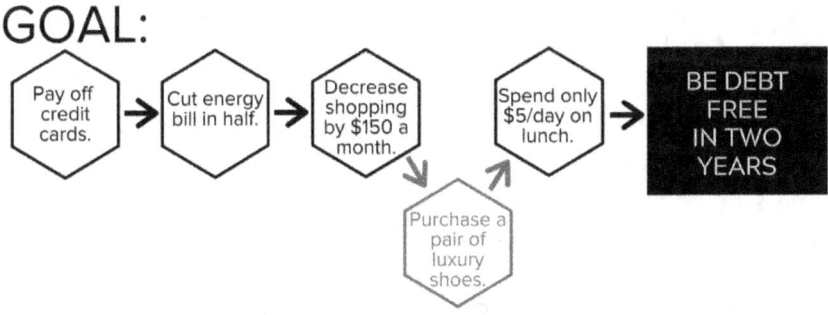

Strategic thinkers understand alignment is critical to building momentum. Strategic thinkers also know a good set of core values can provide you the passion, effort, and energy needed to keep building that momentum. When your core values align with your goals, you have a clearer and a faster path to success. This is one of the secrets to reaching your goals faster than you planned. When decisions align with your core values, you won't waste time evaluating those decisions. You will decide quickly and confidently, because you know which choices do, or do not, agree with your core values.

People don't always choose their core values. Some have these values instilled in them by their parents and/or their community. You may already live by strong core values without realizing it. To get a sense of what your core values are, ask yourself what activities bring you the most joy, or what you couldn't live without. What gives your life meaning or what do you want to achieve? Some examples of core values people might have about life include the following:

- Faith in God that all things are working out for your good.

- An unwavering belief in family first.

- A belief that honesty is the best policy.

- A belief in maintaining a healthy lifestyle.

Surprisingly, developing core values can be fun and will result in a sense of pride and courage for you and/or your family. While travelling the world, I've come across some amazing people who've turned their core values into call-to-action phrases, mottos, or taglines. Some examples were, "I'm a Jones, and we tell it like it is!" or "Who works harder than the Smiths? Nobody!" While strange at first, I soon realized the unifying power of these phrases.

> *"Strategic thinkers know an inspiring company term, team mission statement, or group battle cry is unifying."*

At cookouts, bowling competitions, or community events, I saw even the smallest family member shouting these phrases when their father hit the softball, or their mother bowled a strike. These families wore jerseys with their name across the back, and some even wore polo shirts with a family crest or logo on their breast pocket. Strategic thinkers know an inspiring company term, team mission statement, or group battle cry is unifying.

For example, African Americans around the country felt a unifying sense of pride watching our culture reimagined on the big screen in the movie *Black Panther* (2017). Throughout the movie, the Wakandans continuously reaffirmed their unity with two simple words: Wakanda forever. Their slogan was rich, simple, and powerful. It was the fruit of their pride, the physical manifestation of their core values. Shout it with me: Wakanda forever!

The strategic power of unity is an immeasurable advantage that is typically only seen in sports or the military. I highly recommend you embrace this unity and core values concept in all aspects of your life. This is especially true for leaders, and even truer for parents. Imagine a louder-than-life yelp of "How 'bout them Johnsons!" every time you or your child did something to advance the family toward your strategic goals. Or, just before you send your child off to school, you remind them "We Williams are leaders—not followers!"

Core values help keep you centered on what's *really* important to you. Additionally, they provide you with a consistent sense of direction and purpose. Without a set of core values, it's difficult to create a mission that aligns with who you *truly* are.

As a strategic thinker, you must develop a vision, and goals that align with your core values. Aligning your goals with your core values prevents you from feeling unfulfilled after you have achieved success. There is no worse feeling than spending a lifetime working toward a goal, then feeling unfulfilled when you finally achieve it.

It's Your Move

To the shock of my strategic planning clients, I always start with a finality exercise. I ask them to write their own eulogies. I am asking you to do the same. This serves two purposes: first, it forces you to face the harsh reality of our expiring time on earth. Secondly, it forces you to evaluate what is really important to you. This is a great way to identify and develop your core values. Let's begin:

Your name here _____ *was a* _____

_____

_____ *who* _____

_____. *He/She* _____

_____. *What we will miss most about them is* _____

_____

What we learned from them most was _____

_____.

Once you are done, please circle the character adjectives in your eulogy. Examples of character adjectives are words that were used to describe you above such as: *loving, gentle, caring, faithful, strong, servant, committed, leadership, etc.* **Note:** If you don't like what you think people will say about you at your funeral, make a commitment to improve in that area.

Write your circled words below:

_____

_____

_____

_____

Now, decide which three circled words are most important to you and create a catchy value-phrase around them. **Note:** Value-phrases should be no longer than ten words. Examples of value-phrases might be

*"Always be **loving**, no matter what!"* or *"Forever **faithful**, even during bad times!"* or *"**Leadership** is not about being right, it's about being fair!"*

Value Phrase _____!

Value Phrase _____!

Value Phrase _____!

Congratulations! These are you new core values. Print them out. Write them down. Memorize them. Share them with your family. Get a t-shirt made. Print business cards. Recite them before school, big games, recitals, spelling bees, etc. Now, you must work to develop a culture built around these core values.

Note: If you are married, I encourage you to both create three personal core values each. Then, use one of your personal core values each for two of your three family core values. For your third family core value, redo the eulogy exercise and just use your family name, instead of your personal name. Finally, as a team, pick one of the circled words to build your value-phrase from. As a bonus, create a family logo or a family crest that best illustrates your core values.

These core values are now the foundation of your strategic thinking. They will help you maintain direction and scope. Additionally, they will help you remember, yes, it's great to win. But, *how* you win is just as important. These values will ensure you maintain both an ethical and moral framework while planning and executing your success.

Wealth is more than money; it is also the passing down of good character and generational values. From this point forward, you must now ask yourself, "How does this move align with my core values?" Now you're thinking strategically!

Let's Play: The Knight

When it comes to your chess set, the knight chess piece is often the defining piece in the set. This piece offers the most chance for variety and uniqueness in a chess set, and it is often the piece with the most detail. When it comes to the game of chess, the knight chess piece is often the favorite piece and most unpredictable piece in the game. Many games have been ended because  of the make-or-break tactics with the knight. The knight chess piece moves in a very mysterious way. Unlike rooks, bishops, or queens, the knight is limited in the number of squares it can move across. In fact, its movement is a very specific movement. The piece moves in a shape similar to the uppercase "L". Here are the specifics:

- The knight piece can move forward, backward, left or right two squares and must then move one square in either perpendicular direction.

- The knight piece can only move to one of up to eight positions on the board.

- The knight piece can move to any position not already inhabited by another piece of the same color.

- The knight piece can skip over any other pieces to reach its destination position.

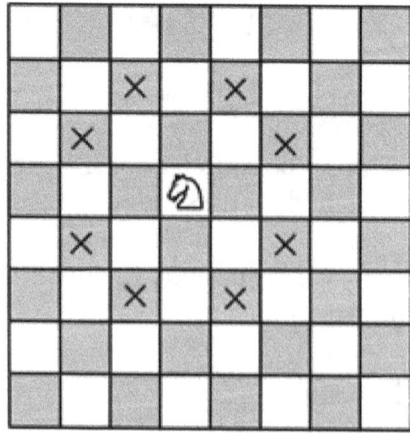

Most experts prefer their knight pieces to be "close to the action". Because of their strange movement, they can often cover weaknesses that other pieces leave. Knight pieces are also best employed near the center of the board, and they are often one of the first pieces to reach the center area. The knight also has a unique ability to attack another piece without risking being attacked by the same piece (aside from other knights, of course).[xxiv]

CHAPTER SIX

DECISION MAKING: THE THREE-MOVE PRINCIPLE™

There are between ten quadrillion vigintillion and one hundred thousand quadrillion vigintillion atoms in the known universe. And guess what? There are more possible moves in a game of chess than there are atoms in the known universe! The moves, choices, and decisions in a single game are unimaginable. Which brings us to our next phase in developing strategic thinking: decision-making.

I remember my stepfather coaching me during chess games. He would say, "One move at a time, one move at a time…" I took that to heart and would place all my focus on that current move. This made perfect sense for a young and beginner chess player. However, I lost way more games than I won; that soon changed.

After a few years, I finally learned a valuable truth. You will never be great at chess if you're just a *one-move* player! If I kept considering my current move as just a single-move, I would always just be in that single moment. Because of my single-move mentality, I always seemed to be at least three moves behind my opponents.

So, I learned to think two to three moves ahead of my current move. This gave me the strategic advantage I was looking for. I began to win in chess, a lot! I call it the Three-Move Principle™. I learned to always ask myself:

1. Are my pieces safe?

2. Do I have any captures?

3. Can my opponent capture any of my pieces?

Like in chess, you will be faced with an impossible number of decisions over your lifetime. As you already know, some decisions are good, and some are bad. What makes a bad decision bad? The outcome. Likewise, what makes a good decision good? The outcome. Therefore, it is crucial to evaluate the potential outcomes for every decision. Here is another secret: by projecting three moves ahead—you can predict the future.

> *"...by projecting three moves ahead—you can predict the future."*

No, you cannot control decision outcomes like magic or time travel, but you can certainly predict outcome probability. Once you figure out what could happen, you can evaluate if you can handle that outcome. When decision-making, you should first determine all possible outcomes, and then, evaluate what results you are not willing to accept.

Before going to college, I asked my daughter how she made decisions. She paused for a second and said, "I consider the outcomes first, and I actually consider the worst outcomes first." I was impressed. We talked at length about first evaluating the *worst-case scenario*.

I shared with her if she worked her way backwards from the worst-case scenario to the decision, she should look for warning signs along the way. These warning signs would serve as reminders for when she was too close to that worst-case scenario. As a result, she could feel free making a riskier decision, because she knows what the "Danger, too close!" signals are. As a result, if she saw these flashing red signals, she should immediately stop and go no further. This is commonly called risk assessment.

On the other hand, if while working your way backward there are no obvious warning-signs, don't do it. You have no emergency exit. You have no way out. In my opinion, if you make it back to the original decision with no available warning-signals, it's a bad choice.

In simple terms, the Three-Move Principle™ is this:

1. If I decide this, what will happen?
2. Then, what will happen?
3. Then, what will happen after that?

Another way of saying it is:

1. I will make this move.
2. But, only to make that move.
3. And then, only to get to that move.

This concept is not rare. Consider all-time hockey great Wayne Gretzky. Gretzky's uncanny ability to read plays is unmatched. The hockey world has yet to produce another player like him. When Gretzky's father (Walter) was asked how his son is so good in hockey, he exclaimed, "Because he never skates to where the puck is, but where it is going!"

Where you are, is not more important than where you are going. Don't live in the moment of the move. You are not being strategic if you don't consider how today's decision affects tomorrow, and the day after that. Don't be a one-move person. When making decisions, use the Three-Move Principle™. This is strategic thinking; this is strategic decision making.

It's Your Move

1. True/False. When decision-making, you should first determine all possible outcomes, and then, evaluate what results you are willing to accept.

2. True/False. By projecting three moves ahead, you can predict the likely outcome.

3. In simple terms, the Three-Move Principle™ is:

_____
_____
_____

    Using the Decision Assistant Checklist© on the next page, please complete the following decision exercise:

- Your dream job just came open at another company.

- You apply.

- After applying, they call and want to interview you next Tuesday at 9 a.m.

- However, you have a very important meeting at 9 a.m. at your current job on the same day.

- You cannot miss this meeting, or you risk losing your current job.

- Also, this is the only day and time you can interview for your dream job.

The Decision Assistant

- ✓ List your possible decisions.
    - ⇒ Do your decision options and expected outcomes align with your core values? Yes/No?
    - ⇒ Eliminate the decisions and outcomes not aligned with your core values.
- ✓ List worst-case and best-case outcomes for each remaining decision.
- ✓ Are there any solutions that will prevent the worst-case outcomes?
    - ⇒ Are the solutions reasonable?
        - Do your solutions align with your core values?
    - ⇒ Are there any danger signs that can provide you "Do Not Continue" warnings?
- ✓ Seriously consider eliminating decisions that don't have "Don't Continue" warning signs. **Note:** Unless the reward is worth the risk.
- ✓ Eliminate the remaining outcomes you are unwilling to accept.
- ✓ Eliminate the remaining solutions you are unable or unwilling to do.
- ✓ Evaluate remaining decisions, outcomes, and solutions.
- ✓ Make the decision—develop the plan.
- ✓ Follow the plan—monitor progress.
- ✓ Revise or adjust the plan when necessary.

Okay, so what do you do?

Let's Play: The Bishop

The two bishops are the other minor pieces in the game. They sit next to the knights and, just as with the knights, they are worth three pawns each (some grandmasters would value them at about 3.3 pawns, due to how powerful they can be in open positions). Happily, the movement of the bishops, which were originally called elephants, is far easier than the knight. The bishop is the ruler over the diagonals of the chessboard. One of them is light-squared and the other one is dark-squared.

When there are no other pieces in their way, bishops can move in any direction diagonally, as many squares as desired. They can capture any piece along the diagonals, and as they can reach so many squares (they can move from one end of the board right to the other in one move), they can prove very useful, especially when working in tandem.[xxv]

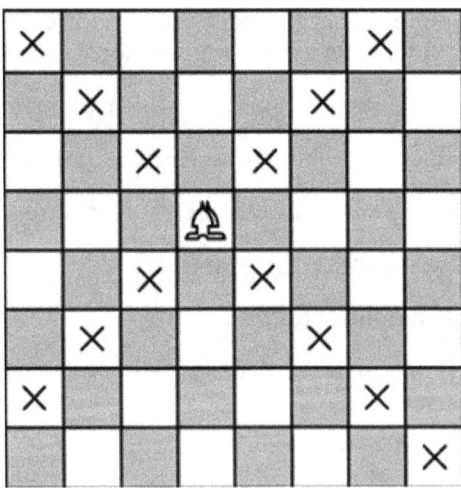

CHAPTER SEVEN

IDENTIFYING STRENGTHS, EMBRACING WEAKNESSES

Great chess players know their weaknesses; this is what makes them great. Even expert chess players are comfortable in the flaws of their game and are continuously working to address their weaknesses. Like great chess players, strategic thinkers are experts in self-awareness. You cannot be great at strategic thinking without a healthy recognition of your deficiencies.

According to Wislow (2017), "Self-awareness is a highly important trait in today's business marketplace. Self-awareness is linked to emotional intelligence, a trait which seems to gain more and more importance for today's big brands."[xxvi] Let's get real: everyone has something they could be doing better. No one is great at everything!

Strategic thinkers don't waste time pretending they know something they don't. They are comfortable admitting they're wrong and are honest about their limitations. However, acknowledging error and limitations is not enough. Strategic thinkers create solutions to correct these errors. Oftentimes, by seeking the help of an expert, a contract professional, or a friend (thought-partner).

Thought-partners are people who care about your success, and you care about theirs. This is why strategic thinkers work intently on developing new relationships and sustaining a network of talented friends. You must do the same. When time won't allow you to get the training or experience needed to finish a project, you must leverage or maximize the skills of your thought-partners.

> *"When thought-partners don't have money (investment capital) to give you, they give of their talent."*

As a thought-partner, you, yourself, must be willing to offer services at your bottom-line or even free. During the early or start-up years, this is invaluable. Trust me, this is how it's done. When thought-partners don't have money (investment capital) to give you, they give of their talent. These relationships are strategic and are commonly known as strategic partnerships. This is why you must keep your talented friends close and informed on your projects. As you grow, they grow. As a result, "we all eat!"

I learned this best from former all-pro quarterback and NFL great Randall Cunningham. He taught me the power of collaboration, and the value of having smart and talented friends. Randall is quite honestly the most strategic human being I have ever met in my life. Trust me when I tell you, success is no accident in the Cunningham household. It's expected. It's planned. It's strategic.

You see, whether you realize it or not, African Americans are masters of collaboration (think family reunion). We must revive our tribal nature— our roots. We must realize we are stronger together. But first, we must be willing to admit we need help. To become an expert strategist, you must be vulnerable and transparent. Admitting your imperfections creates trust within your network.

A colleague of mine once offered me some amazing advice. She looked me in my eyes and said, "Dorian, excellence is not perfection." I took this to heart, because I know I suffer from "redo-itis." Redo-itis (re-doo-eye-tis) is when you never think your work is complete or good enough. As a result, you miss deadlines or even worse, don't submit anything at all.

For example, as a young Air Force Major, I was tasked with rewriting the curriculum for USAF Pilot Training. This was an enormous project with high visibility. As a matter of fact, the training program's past failures were brought before a congressional committee and aired on live television. This paralyzed me, as I thought, "Wow, if this fails, they will talk about me like that!" I went into overdrive. I worked relentlessly to ensure the courseware was perfect.

Even after long nights and stressful days, the new courseware was never good enough for me to say, "It is finished!" I kept redoing it, and redoing it, and redoing it again. After missing several deadlines, I finally got it done. I was overwhelmed with the fear of negative comments and a general lack of acceptance. I reluctantly published the new courseware. Right on cue, I received a dozen emails and phone calls from senior leaders and colleagues.

> *"...if you have to keep redoing something, it's not your strength."*

Honestly, their comments were justified and in *most* cases, absolutely correct. During the review process, my boss and I noticed a trend: the criticism pointed to the same areas of animation-graphic design, and training relevance. It was then I realized, I never asked for help in the areas I was admittingly deficient in.

For that project, I failed to identify my weak areas. And, what made this so ridiculous was that I had the world's best pilots, graphic designers, and animators just a few cubicles down from me. Duh—had I included them in the process, I would have slept better, had fewer migraines, and released a better product the first time. My wife, who is my most trusted mentor and thought-partner, will attest to the countless times I should have just "asked for help."

Redo-itis is the result of one thing: a severe lack of self-awareness. It is a sickness, the result of arrogance, denial, and pride. Newsflash: There was only one perfect person to ever live, and it *ain't* any of us. Here's another secret—if you have to keep redoing something, it's not your strength. Get help! *Just saying.*

Here is where we must get real. In my opinion, we, as African Americans, undervalue the advice of experts. We try to do *it* ourselves, even when *we* have never done *it* before. For almost three-decades, I've led thousands of diverse people, managed billions of dollars in resources and capital, and have worked with best-selling authors, professional and Olympic athletes, politicians, and all education levels. I can assure you this; we, as African Americans, are not short on work ethic, skill, talent, intellect, courage, and grit. However, I have noticed one commonly glaring weakness: we don't like to admit we have a weakness.

This is not an indictment on us as a people; it's a common truth I have observed first-hand. Unfortunately, this, too, is the result of our self-perception as people of color, and the "one strike and you're out" truth that exists in the social, economic, and even the entertainment sectors. We have all been told, "…you must be twice as good just to be average" (Every Black Momma and Daddy in America, n.d.). Sorry America, whether you like it or not, this is a fact. Here is an excerpt from an eye-opening article (2015) by *The Atlantic* on this issue:[xxvii]

"…you must be twice as good just to be average."

"Didn't you know that black people don't get a second chance?"

Prince, 2014

"Research from the National Bureau of Economic Research shows that black workers receive extra scrutiny from bosses, which can lead to worse performance reviews, lower wages, and even job loss. The data also found that the pool of unemployed black workers is likely to be seen as less skilled because of more consistent or prolonged unemployment. That can make companies less likely to hire them, and more skeptical once they do."

This leads employers to invest more heavily in monitoring black employees. That could be everything from instructing supervisors to closely watch a new hire, or more directly monitoring job performance.

The report goes on to say, "Because black workers are more closely scrutinized, it increases the chances that errors—large or small—will be caught. According to the researchers, it's more likely that a black employee would be let go for these errors than a white one."

Lang (2015) says, "…blacks simply don't get a second chance. Once fired, black workers return to the pool of unemployed—where they will once again have a difficult time finding work, prompting their next employer to be wary as well. In the meantime, white workers are less scrutinized, and as a result, they enjoy a longer tenure on the job, which leads to a stronger work history, more skills, and higher wages" (TheAtlantic.com).

The entertainment industry is no different. During an interview,[xvviii] the late-great Prince Rogers Nelson criticized the music business, explaining, "It's box office. I can't have something like *The Great Gatsby* on my hands. Didn't you know that black people don't get a second chance?" It's like Chris Rock said: Leonardo DiCaprio can make one bad movie after another, and he just keeps going. Chris Rock makes a bad movie, and he doesn't work again. Black people aren't allowed to make mistakes.

I could go on for days, months, and years, using statistical analysis and emerging trends to further prove this point. And if this book weren't written for people of color, I would probably have to. But it's not—**IT IS** written for us. And we don't need descriptive or inferential statistics to prove something we live every single day. We are fully aware; as African Americans, we probably won't get a second chance if we mess up.

As a result, we don't easily admit we don't know something or that we have a weakness. This is especially true in corporate America, where stereotypes and biases are ever-present. There are countless times I have been in a conversation or a meeting and had absolutely no clue what we were talking about. I just nodded my head smartly, took copious notes, and afterwards, scurried to my desk to do a Google search. After all, I was the first black man to ever get this job—I was the first one in the history of the entire USAF. I wasn't going to acknowledge my weakness. No way!

But, here's the problem. When we don't acknowledge our weaknesses, we can't get the help we need to overcome our deficiencies. This is a true *catch-22*, but there is a strategy that can help. This strategy is known as the strengths, weaknesses, opportunities, and threats (SWOT) analysis.

"...you should perform a SWOT analysis at least once a year."

The exact origin of the SWOT is hotly debated. Many claim it was developed in the 1950s at Harvard Business School by professors George Albert Smith, Jr. and Kenneth Andrews. Others proclaim it was the work Albert S. Humphrey in the 1960s at the Stanford Research Institute. Regardless of its creator, the SWOT analysis is arguably today's most widely used strategic planning tool.

A SWOT analysis is a tool used to provide leaders a new perspective on what the company does well, where its challenges are, and which direction to go. Likewise, a personal SWOT analysis will provide you the same data. Accomplishing a good SWOT analysis will help you avoid those "I don't know" situations by identifying areas where you need improvement. Additionally, in areas where you are just not that great (like my earlier graphic-design example), you can proactively hire a coach, expert, consultant, or get help from a thought-partner. In other words, you can say, "I don't know" on your own terms and in a strategic and proactive way.

As a strategic thinker and planner, you should perform a SWOT analysis at least once a year. You should also conduct one when there is a significant change or a life-altering event, such as a new job, new baby, pregnancy, divorce, marriage, loss of life, etc.

Lastly, a SWOT will help you dodge the *no second chances* dilemma in both your personal and your professional life. A personal SWOT analysis is your go-to strategic tool.

It's Your Move

1. True/False. Like great chess players, strategic thinkers are experts in self-awareness.

2. True/False. You cannot be great at strategic thinking without a healthy recognition of your deficiencies.

3. In your own words, describe how you personally feel about admitting your weaknesses to other people?

4. True/False. According to research, because black workers are more closely scrutinized, it increases the chances that errors—large or small—will be caught.

5. Redo-itis is the result of one thing, a severe lack of _____.

6. True/False. If you have to keep redoing something, it's not your strength.

7. In areas where you could improve, you should:

    a. Proactively hire a coach, expert or a consultant.

    b. Be quiet about it and hope no one sees.

    c. Wait until someone teaches you how to get better at it.

    d. Hire an expert to do the work you are weak in.

    e. Leverage the talent of you thought-partners.

    f. Do a, d, and e.

    g. None of the above.

Let's Play: The Queen

The Queen, with a crown on her head, is (besides the king!) the most important and powerful piece in the game of chess. Each player has just one queen and she is worth nine pawns!

The queen sits next to the bishop – on the central square that matches the piece's color (a black queen starts on the black square in the middle of all the other pieces, a white queen on a white square).

As she has the widest reach of all pieces, she can become the most dangerous member of the game for your opponents. It is essential to protect her and use her effectively at the same time.

For most players, the loss of the queen means the loss of the whole game. So, always be careful with your Queen, as she is unique.

She can move in any direction and any number of squares. The one thing she can't do is jump over other pieces. The Queen can capture any of the opponent's pieces that are in her way. This piece is very useful for different kinds of tactics and attacks. Be careful not to bring your queen out into the open too soon, as you may find her in danger from the opponent's pieces.[xxix]

CHAPTER EIGHT

HOW TO CONDUCT A PERSONAL SWOT ANALYSIS

First and foremost, there are a host of strategic planning models and frameworks. Of those hundreds, there are some very popular and well-used models. Below are four examples of these varying models or frameworks:

Balanced Scorecard—The Balanced Scorecard (BSC) was originally developed by Dr. Robert Kaplan, of Harvard University, and Dr. David Norton as a framework for measuring organizational performance using a more BALANCED set of performance measures.

Porter's Five Forces—This tool was created by Harvard Business School professor Michael Porter. He created this concept to analyze an industry's attractiveness and likely profitability. Since its publication in 1979, it has become one of the most popular and highly regarded business strategy tools. Porter recognized that organizations likely keep a close watch on their rivals, but he encouraged them to look beyond the actions of their competitors and examine what other factors could impact the business environment. He identified five forces that make up the competitive environment, and which can erode your profitability.

OKR—The acronym OKR stands for Objectives and Key Results, a popular goal management framework that helps companies implement strategy. The benefits of the framework include improved focus, increased transparency, and better alignment.

SWOT Analysis—A "SWOT" analysis is an incredibly simple, yet powerful tool to help you develop your business strategy, whether you're building a startup or guiding an existing company. I recommend the SWOT analysis tool; this is my strategic planning framework of choice. Heinz Weihrich created a 2 x 2 matrix to provide a way to write out the answers to the four key questions for easy comparison. Strengths and weaknesses were across the top, and opportunities and threats in the bottom row. This remains the most common and effective way to conduct the analysis. There are many formats for the SWOT analysis; the four-quadrant matrix below is the most common:

Strengths	Weaknesses
Opportunities	Threats

According to Martin (2019), strengths and opportunities are things you consider favorable and within your control, while weaknesses and threats are unfavorable and dictated by external forces. You can use these definitions to explore the correlation between your strengths and weaknesses, how to leverage your strengths to make the most of your opportunities, and how to improve weaknesses to mitigate threats.[xxx] When conducting a personal SWOT analysis, you should always think about why you are doing it.

Also, think about what you want? Examples might be:

- I want/need a promotion.
- I want to grow personally.
- I need to recover from my divorce.
- I need to prepare for the birth of my twins.
- I want to leave my job to pursue my dream job (see the earlier example from Chapter 6: *It's Your Move*).

A SWOT analysis will help you identify:

1. What will help you get there?
2. What will stop you from getting there?
3. Who is helping you get there?
4. Who is stopping you from getting there?
5. What you need to do about numbers 1 through 4.

To conduct an analysis, ask yourself questions about each of the four examined areas with respect to your reason for conducting the analysis. Be honest! Honesty is crucial for the analysis to generate meaningful results. With that in mind, try to see yourself from the standpoint of a colleague or a bystander, and view criticism with objectivity. If you are really serious, have a colleague, your spouse, your child, or a thought-partner complete a SWOT analysis on you. The following *how-to* is excerpted from Mindtools® Personal SWOT Analysis:[xxxi] These are some basic questions to help you start to develop a SWOT framework:

Strengths

- What advantages do you have that others don't have (for example, skills, certifications, education, or connections)?
- What do you do better than anyone else?

- What personal resources can you access?
- What do other people (and your boss, in particular) see as your strengths?
- Which of your achievements are you most proud of?
- What values do you believe in that others fail to exhibit?
- Are you part of a network that no one else is involved in? If so, what connections do you have with influential people?

Weaknesses

- What tasks do you usually avoid because you don't feel confident doing them?
- What will the people around you see as your weaknesses?
- Are you completely confident in your education and skills training? If not, where are you weakest?
- What are your negative work habits (for example, are you often late, are you disorganized, do you have a short temper, or are you poor at handling stress)?
- Do you have personality traits that hold you back in your field? For instance, if you have to conduct meetings on a regular basis, a fear of public speaking would be a major weakness.

Opportunities

- What new technology can help you? Or can you get help from others or from people via the Internet?
- Is your industry growing? If so, how can you take advantage of the current market?
- Do you have a network of strategic contacts to help you, or offer good advice?

- What trends (management or otherwise) do you see in your company, and how can you take advantage of them?
- Are any of your competitors failing to do something important? If so, can you take advantage of their mistakes?
- Is there a need in your company or industry that no one is filling?
- Do your customers or vendors complain about something in your company? If so, could you create an opportunity by offering a solution?

You will also find useful opportunities in the following:

⇒ Networking events, educational classes, or conferences.

⇒ A colleague going on an extended leave. Could you take on some of this person's projects to gain experience?

⇒ A new role or project that forces you to learn new skills, like public speaking or international relations.

⇒ A company expansion or acquisition. Do you have specific skills (like a second language) that could help with the process?

Threats

- What obstacles do you currently face at work?
- Are any of your colleagues competing with you for projects or roles?
- Is your job (or the demand for the things you do) changing?
- Does changing technology threaten your position?
- Could any of your weaknesses lead to threats?

It's Your Move

We have covered a lot of ground so far. Let's review:

- Chapter One—Introduction to Strategic Thinking.
- Chapter Two—Why for Write a Book for African Americans?
- Chapter Three—Inequity versus Inequality.
- Chapter Four—You is Smart, You is Kind, You is Important!
- Chapter Five—Developing Your Core Values.
- Chapter Six—Decision Making: The Three-Move Principle™.
- Chapter Seven—Identifying Strengths, Embracing Weaknesses.
- Chapter Eight—How to Conduct a Personal SWOT Analysis.

Now it's time to start applying your new strategic thinking skills. It's time for you to conduct your own personal SWOT analysis. You are more than ready for this. Please remember to be brutally honest, and remember, this analysis will help propel you to greatness. However, this is not just your standard SWOT analysis. This analysis will include solutions to your self-evaluations. You will have a SWOTlution™!

In my opinion, it is not strategic to conduct a SWOT analysis without developing solutions. These solutions are the beginning of transitioning you from a strategic thinker into a strategic planner. Remember, vulnerability and transparency are the most valuable traits of a strategic thinkers. Let's Go!

On the next page is a **SWOTlution**™. The difference between the SWOTlution™ and other SWOT quadrants is the addition of four solution quadrants to make eight squares, instead of four. You will use this tool later, so make sure you really understand how to use it.

Note: This version is small, due to the size of the book pages. For this exercise, please use a standard 8.5 X 11 piece of paper (sideways or landscape) to give yourself enough space to clearly write and brainstorm. You can also download a full-page version at www.StrategyBrother.com:

The Purpose of this SWOTlution™ is—	
Positive	Negative
STRENGTHS 1	WEAKNESSES 2
• _____ _____ • _____ _____ • _____ _____	• _____ _____ • _____ _____ • _____ _____
SOLUTIONS TO GET STRONGER	SOLUTIONS TO MY WEAKNESSES
• _____ _____ • _____ _____ • _____	• _____ _____ • _____ _____ • _____

STRATEGIC PLANNING

OPPORTUNITIES 3	THREATS 4
• _____ _____ • _____ _____ • _____ _____	• _____ _____ • _____ _____ • _____ _____
SOLUTIONS TO MY OPPORTUNITIES	**SOLUTIONS TO MY THREATS**
• _____ _____ • _____ _____ • _____ _____	• _____ _____ • _____ _____ • _____ _____

Figure 8.1, SWOTlution™

Let's Play: The King

The King is the most important piece in any chess game and is placed next to the Queen, wearing a cross on his head. He is worth endless pawns, the lives of all your other pieces, because when you checkmate the opponent's King, the game is over, and you carry home a victory! Thus, it is crucial to keep your king safe and try to weaken the opponent's King.

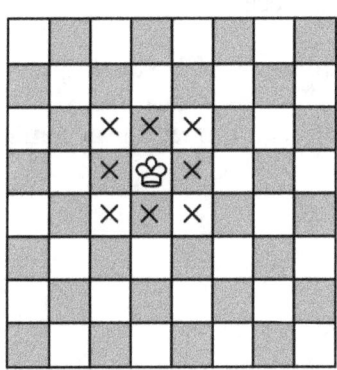

The King is limited in his movement. He can move just one square in any direction, but only if he isn't placed in check by doing so. The king can participate in a special move called "castling". When you castle, you simultaneously move your king and one of your rooks. Thereby, you move the king two squares towards your rook and then move the rook to the square over which the king crossed (be sure to do it in this order – if you move your rook first, it's counted as a normal rook move and you'll lose the chance to castle). In chess, there are two types of castling:

1. Castling on the kingside (often called castling short).

2. Castling on the queenside (often called castling long).

Castling might sound complicated in theory, but let's see how easy it is in practice. However, there are a number of rules when castling is possible and when not. You can only castle, if:

1. Your king has not moved in the game yet.

2. Your king is not in check.

3. The king does not castle through a square, which is controlled by an opponent's piece.

4. The king is not in check after castling.

5. The rook has not been moved in the game yet.[xxxii]

CHAPTER NINE

TURNING YOUR DREAM INTO A VISION

I can dream of being great at chess, but at some point, I must decide to become great. The decision to try and achieve your dream is the beginning of a vision. A vision is what you'll look like after you've achieved your dream. Some people don't realize dreams are just promises of what *could* happen, but not visions. Visions are dreams that have *already* happened. Dreams are only possibilities—visions are prophetic. Real talk—we need fewer dreamers and more visionaries.

A dream is where potential dies, vision is where it lives. Dreaming of being great at something is not enough. If it doesn't inspire you, it will become your nightmare. Unfortunately, no strategy in the world can truly inspire you. Don't stop dreaming until you discover what inspires you.

In an article by John Vogt (2019), he states, "When we call someone a dreamer, it is rarely a compliment. We generally mean someone who is unfocused or lost in their own thoughts, and we expect that they are unlikely to do anything of value or to make any meaningful impact." In no way am I suggesting that dreaming is bad, it's that the transition from a dreamer to a visionary can be more challenging than some think.

When we label someone a visionary, it is an entirely different compliment. "They are someone we see as ahead of their time, bold and adventurous. We expect them to do great things. The difference is they make things happen here in the real world." xxxiii

Okay, here is where is gets difficult. Let's say a novice chess player enters a chess match. He is confident because he's won several tournaments against other people from his local chess club. He has dreams of winning and dreams of being the youngest player to ever win this tournament.

He sits down to play and realizes his opponent is Ding Liren, the highest rated player in China and two-time Olympic Champion. The chance of this novice getting a win against Liren is virtually impossible. It doesn't mean it *can't* happen; it's just highly unlikely. The novice must do the best he can, for as long as he can.

> *"People who are afraid of second opinions already have their minds made up."*

In this case, this novice chess player allowed his dreams to drive his actions. He never worked to turn his dream into a vision. We must not be afraid to put our dreams under intense scrutiny. You must at least check to see if your dream can survive the SWOTlution™ and a core value alignment evaluation.

I recommend getting your thought-partners or mentors to give you honest feedback on your dreams. Remember, you may have a bias, and the dream may be affecting your better judgment. Don't be afraid of getting a second opinion. People who are afraid of second opinions already have their minds made up. They realize it's not the best decision, but don't want to hear about it.

For example, my senior year in high school, I believed I would one day play in the NFL. I was fast, quick, and fearless. However, I was a 135-pound bag of feathers and never really recovered from a compound leg fracture just three years before. Was it possible for me to play in the NFL? Sure. Was it likely? No.

I'm not saying you should give up on your athletic or entertainment dreams. I am simply saying, conduct a SWOTlution™ with your mentor, and then, deal with the truth before you start developing a strategy. Here's yet another secret to success—the SWOTlution™ process will force you to consider the difficulty of transforming your dream into a vision.

After my senior football season in high school, my coach handed me a dozen or so recruitment letters and said to me, "Son, I love you, and you're tough as nails, but you are too light in the britches to play at these schools, and you always seem a little timid when running up the middle of the defense...you should really focus on track." We both cried, and then we both laughed—uncontrollably. I then finally admitted to him that I was still deathly afraid to get my leg hit. Two months later, I accepted a full-athletic scholarship in track and field.

Looking back, I'm grateful for my coach's honesty. However, he failed. It wasn't what he said that I attribute to failure; it was what he didn't say. He never offered me a strategy to work on my weaknesses. He also failed to realize I was a lost and scared young black kid who was one decision away from selling drugs like my *pops*.

My grades were terrible, I was sleeping on the floor of my cousin's room, and I had zero plans outside of football. My childhood friends were living that "gang life", and I absolutely hated track—I only ran for the girls. You see, where I'm from, most of us didn't have college funds or wealthy parents. So, what I needed from my coach was a strategy, not a dang talent observation.

"...achieving success is not a 'faith' issue; it's an obedience issue."

This happens far too often to young, talented black kids with a tough home life. First, we let other people use us for our talent. Then, we put all our eggs into this ...*music thing* or this ...*getting to the league thing*. Newsflash: we do more than just run and jump, or sing and dance!

By the way, just a year later, I flunked out of college and lost my scholarship—weed, women, and wine. Like I said, I hated track. What I needed was a strategy, not a monthly stipend, a set of starting blocks, and no oversight. So, to all the coach, teacher, principal, and pastor-

STRATEGIC PLANNING

type people out there, when you offer a harsh truth, also offer a strategic alternative. Black kids have been hearing and seeing harsh truths their whole lives—all you're doing is corroborating our plight by stating the obvious.

Let me take this moment and speak to the "all things by faith" discussion. As a pastor and man of faith, I certainly believe in signs, miracles, and wonders. As a matter of fact, I have seen them with my own two eyes. I also believe faith is the substance of things hoped for and the evidence of things unseen. However, I also believe what people try to *use* their *faith* for is largely self-centered and not always in the best interest of the kingdom.

You see, achieving success is not a faith issue; it's an obedience issue. Many of us have amazing, wonderful, and sometimes far-fetched dreams. However, when God inspires us with a vision that doesn't include those dreams, we rebel. Many even say, "nah, that can't be God!" As a result, we keep trying to *faith* our way to what we truly want—not what He has directed us to achieve. For-real for-real, *"Did God really say?"* (Genesis 3:1, KJV).

It's Your Move

Now that you understand a vision versus a dream, let's do the first step to actual personal strategic planning, **FILTER YOUR DREAMS AND DEVELOP YOUR VISION.**

1. Using the space below, please brainstorm and list all your dreams. Next, circle your top three dreams. **Helpful Tip:** Only circle the dreams you feel like you must accomplish before you die.

_____

_____

2. If it's career-related, ask yourself, "Would I do this for free?"

   Yes or No

3. If you would not do this for free, you need to need stop, pray, and reflect on your core values. **Helpful Tip:** If you did not actually think through the core values exercise, go back to Chapter 5 and redevelop your core values.

Coaching Moment: If there's nothing you'd do for free, don't fret; earning potential (becoming wealthy) can be a great motivator. However, this is a slippery slope, and you could get stuck in a materialism trap. Try really hard to determine a life passion, such as helping people succeed, assisting the previously incarcerated with re-entry support, helping the underserved and under-resourced, etc.

It takes money to do all of this. So, if your dream is to become wealthy so you can personally fund worthy nonprofits, companies or initiatives, you should embrace that! You are needed.

4. Why do you want to achieve this dream? Does your *why* align with your core values?

_____

_____

5. What will happen if you don't achieve this dream?

_____

_____

6. Which three below will be the most affected if you don't achieve this dream? This information will help you when you start your research and professional development.

   a. Homeless, hungry, underserved, those living in poverty (Social Sector)

   b. Those discriminated against, such as women, minorities, senior citizens, the LGBT+ community (Equity & Human Rights Sector)

   c. You, your children and grandchildren, your family, and your friends (Personal Sector)

   d. Sellers, shoppers, buyers, bankers, business owners and entrepreneurs, fashion and makeup experts (Retail Sector)

   e. Healthcare professionals, sick and ailing, cancer patients, those with incurable diseases (Healthcare & Healthy Living Sector)

f. Students, teachers, school administrators, schools and universities, trade schools, and adult learning programs (Education and Training Sector)

g. Grocers, farmers, water treatment and hydro experts, restaurants and food servicers (Food and Agricultural Sector)

h. Military, Department of Defense, government workers, civil service employees (National Defense Industry)

i. Other:

7. Accomplish a decision analysis on this dream. Is pursuing this dream a good decision? If it's a bad decision, have the courage to go back to #1 and choose another dream. **Note:** Get a second opinion and then, deal with the truth. This is where we fail— WE DON'T LIKE THE TRUTH. If it's a good decision, move on to #8.

8. When you accomplish this dream, will you be happy, fulfilled, and satisfied? No? Start over at #1. If the answer is "yes", move on to the next question.

9. Translate your dream into a vision and a mission. Remember, a vision is what you will be—not what you will do. When developing your vision, it is helpful to visualize what you will look like after you achieve your dream. **Note:** A mission is what your work looks like to accomplish your vision. It's the physical work, the thing you do.

- For example, your **vision** might be to become the first black woman to become a Supreme Court justice. Remember, your vision is what you want to be—what you want to become.

- Along with your vision, you will need to craft a mission. Your mission is what you want to do.

  ⇒ Your **mission** might be to provide a positive role model for other discriminated groups of people. To expose unfair and restricting systems of inequity within our local, state, regional, and national judiciary systems. So, remember, your mission is what you want to do.

STRATEGIC PLANNING

You must make sure your vision and mission are S.M.A.R.T. The S.M.A.R.T. principle is a strategic tool that will help keep you honest. SMART is an acronym that stands for **Specific, Measurable, Achievable, Realistic, and Timely.** Using the SMART principle ensures your vision and mission makes good strategic sense. As a result, your vision will have strategic scope or genuine boundaries. Here is a quick summary of each of the SMART Principles:

- **Specific:** Well-defined, clear, and unambiguous
- **Measurable:** With specific criteria that measure your progress towards the accomplishment of the vision.
- **Achievable:** Attainable and not impossible to achieve.
- **Realistic:** Within reach, realistic, and relevant to your life purpose.
- **Timely:** With a clearly defined timeline, including a starting date and a target date. The purpose is to create urgency.

Coaching Moment: You should work to develop a vision and mission for each major area of your life, such as parenting, marriage, career, spiritual, economic, etc. You should also target a certain time (1-year, 5-year, 10-year, etc.) to accomplish your vision and mission. I tried to tell you—don't "nobody" have time for 30 hours of TV per week! Here is an example of my **career** vision and mission:

- **(20-Year) Vision:** By 2025 and until 2041, I will be the city's leader and go-to expert in racial reconciliation and equity programming.

- **(20-Year) Mission:** Until 2041, through mentoring and intervention programs—I will work to increase minority-owned SATX businesses and nonprofits by 10 percent annually. I will work to decrease college dropout rates by 5 percent annually for at risk-students in "Distressed Community" zip codes. My family and I will continue this fight until San Antonio is at, or above, the national average for minority-owned business/nonprofits and post-secondary graduation rates for at-risk students.

- **(2041 and Beyond):** I will retire at 65 years of age and travel with my wife, serving where I'm needed. I will spend the rest of my days teaching my grandchildren to teach their grandchildren who they are.

Now it's your turn:

Write your vision here:

_____
_____
_____
_____

Write your mission here:

_____
_____
_____
_____

Write your core values here:

_____
_____
_____
_____

Let's Play: Starting the Game

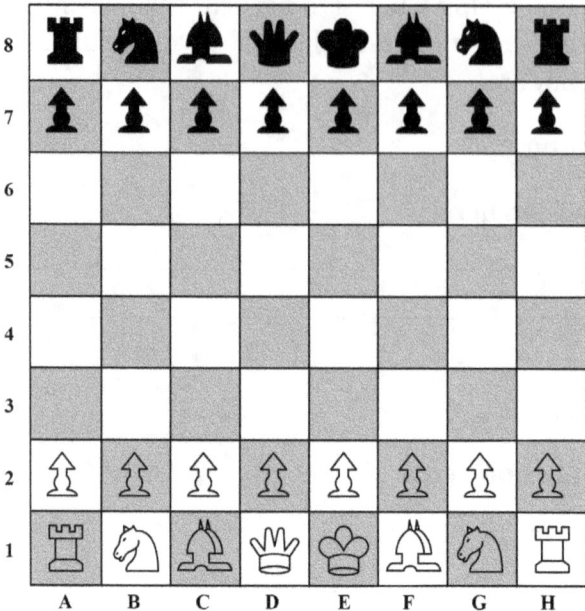

Setup. The board is setup as shown. There should always be a white square at the closest right-hand side for both players. The queen must be on a square that matches her color.

Turns or Moves. A move is the act of moving one chess piece to another square. White always moves first, and players alternate turns. Players can only move one piece at a time, except when castling. Remember each piece has its own type of move (e.g. the bishop only moves diagonally).

Taking Pieces or Capturing. A capture is done by moving to the square where your opponent's piece is—then physically removing it from the board. You cannot capture your own piece. Players take pieces when they encounter an opponent in their movement path. Only pawns take differently than they move (pawns move forward but capture diagonally one space). Players cannot capture their own pieces.[xxxiv]

CHAPTER TEN

GATHER THE FACTS, GET THE INFORMATION

When first introduced to chess, I approached it like I approached checkers. I tried to attack everything in front of me and just hoped to somehow get to the king. I had no real strategy; I had done no real research on how to play. Then, I met one of my stepdad's *associates* who owned a "rug store." Rug-Man and my stepdad would sometimes "work" out of this "rug store" and play chess in between "customers". This dude should have been a master chess player. He dominated both my stepdad and me regularly.

There was one game I will never forget. After every move I made, he said, "Well, that was dumb!" My stepdad would repeat after him with, "yep—dumb." This went on for two hours before I broke into tears and wanted to quit.

Feeling sorry for me, Rug-Man handed me an old book that looked like it had been through hell and back. It was rolled-up, dirty, and looked like it was once used as a dustpan. You know, when you don't have a dustpan and you have to wet the end of the paper so it sticks to the floor? Never mind.

"Strategic thinkers know there is always something they don't know."

This book was titled *Bobby Fischer Teaches Chess*, (Fischer, 1982). Rug-Man told me to read it twice front to back, then come back and play him again when I was ready. I read that book three times on the first day, alone. In my opinion, Fischer's book is the *one* for beginner chess players to read. I say this because it doesn't just cover the chess pieces and their movements; it empowers you with scenarios, concepts, themes, and overall strategy of the game, itself. After I read this book, neither the Rug-Man, nor my stepdad ever beat me again! All it took was a little research. Truth is—*folks* get nervous when you start reading.

I soon realized that old and beaten up book, was the primary reason their chess games were better than mine. Then one day, like a scene out of a movie, they both said to me, "Don't you ever again wait for someone to give you the information you need—go get it yourself." I never forgot that; neither should you.

Strategic thinkers know there is always something they don't know. They then work relentlessly to find out what they're missing—where's that rolled-up book? As a strategic thinker, you must never stop at "I don't know." You must work tirelessly to gather the facts and to get the information. At this point, you already have a vision, a mission, core values, and you are ready to pursue your future. You have worked too hard to just guess. Don't blow it by acting like you know something you don't (See Chapter 7, *Identifying Strengths, Embracing Weaknesses*).

You must find out what it's *really* going to take to achieve your goals. Now, much of *how* you research depends on *why* and *what* you research. If your vision is to become a better mother, then this is largely framed around the *Personal Sector*. Your sector determines where you research, and what industry you need to become an expert in. If you don't know what sector your vision falls into, please go back and review Chapter 9, *Knowing a Dream vs. a Vision*.

So, if your dream is to become a better mother? Much of your research should revolve around reading books on maternity, listening to woman-mother centered podcasts, creating or joining a network of winning mothers, seeking a mentor or life coach, or maybe you, yourself, might get a certification in life coaching or mentoring.

Next, you must empower your primary stakeholders to monitor your work and evaluate your progress. In this case, your primary stakeholders would be your children…lol! Don't forget, in order to keep a manageable scope, you must first define what a better mother even looks like. What was your vision in the first place? Remember, no matter how boring or time consuming this is, you cannot skip steps. In strategic planning, every move counts.

What you don't do in the early stages will come back to haunt you. What you don't define at the beginning of the strategic planning process will become a showstopper. Be patient and do it right the first time. This will save you time and money.

It's now time for you to conduct your research. Ultimately, your research results will provide you with what it takes to achieve your vision. All research starts with a question or a statement. In 1996, my statement was, "After my Air Force career is over, I want to coach, mentor, and pastor people to be their best selves. However, the social and spiritual sector doesn't pay much."

As a result, my question ended up being, "How can I obtain sustainable wealth and still help people?" **Note:** I defined sustainable wealth as a six-figure salary for the rest of my life. I then conducted all my research based on this above question-statement. So, what is your question or statement? For example:

- How do I become the first African-American female chief justice?
- How can I get my book published?
- What do Registered Nurses make annually?
- What type of education must I have to become a pilot?
- How do my children become Merit Scholars?
- How much money do I need to start a fast-food franchise?
- How much money does a probation officer make?
- How can I become a sports agent?

Good research is what helps you discover what it takes to become your vision. For example, if you want to enter a certain career field, you must first find out "how?" You must determine what current employers are asking for, or what it takes to enter the market as a business owner.

There are thousands of tools to you can use when researching what its *really* going to take to achieve your goals. However, I'm only going to focus on the following tools:

1. The Internet
2. The Big Three
3. Strategic Networking

The Internet. I believe the Internet is the single greatest strategic planning tool ever created. It is user-friendly, and in most cases, you can find out exactly what you need to achieve your goals—for free. This was not always the case. The Internet wasn't mainstream until 1990. Before that, research and analysis looked a little like this:

- If you wanted to find out what classes you needed to take get an undergraduate degree, you had to get your hands on an academic catalog, or you had to schedule a face-to-face with an academic advisor.

- If you wanted to research how much companies were paying entry-level administrative professionals, you had to look in the newspaper (Want Ads) or know someone on the inside.

- You can now even get a high school diploma or PhD all on the Internet!

Employment job search websites are powerful tools for career planning. For example, let's say you desire to become a Chief Financial Officer (CFO); you can simply search the U.S. Department of Labor, or one of the many employment sites. There, you will find the information you are looking for such as:

- Education requirements
- Experience requirements

- Certification requirements

- Compensation and benefits

- Knowledge, Skills, and Assessments (KSAs)

It doesn't get any easier than this. Looking back on it, the amount of hustling African Americans had to do before the Internet was simply amazing. Our great trailblazers understood the necessity of strategic planning, and they did it well. In their cases, racism wasn't just systemic—it was legal.

Even with the odds against them, the mainstream was still forced to deal with the likes Thurgood Marshall, Robert Abbot, Alvin Ailey, Muhammad Ali, Richard Allen, and Maya Angelou. No social media. No website. No search engine. So, for everyone who was strategic planning and climbing sector ladders before the Internet was invented—we applaud you!

The Big Three—What I'm getting ready to tell you is not rocket science, however, this advice has helped countless people achieve their goals and eventually break through the glass ceiling. FYI: The glass ceiling is "those artificial barriers based on attitudinal or organizational bias that prevent qualified individuals from advancing upward in their organization into management-level positions."

There are three big areas you must maximize if you want to break through the glass ceiling—education, experience, and certification.

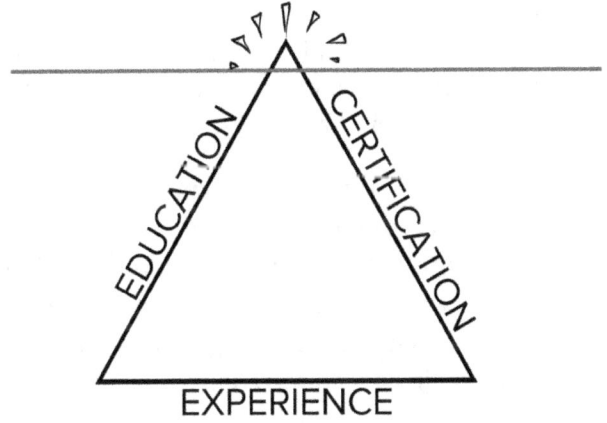

Education. Researching education requirements is a major part of the work you must accomplish when considering a career or hobby. It is important to understand whether a certain level or type of degree or diploma is required. There are two terms you should look for when conducting your research those terms are *preferred* or *required*.

Certain jobs or careers may require a high school diploma or a G.E.D., while others will require a terminal degree (e.g. PhD). This kind of research must be done on the front end, before you start working toward a career. This is extremely important, as certain careers are not as cut and dry as physicians or dentists. Some careers or job postings may have more vague education requirements, such as *"Bachelor's degree preferred in one of the following areas: education, marketing, business, leadership, or humanities."*

You must know what education is *required* and what type is *preferred*. This information must be gathered early in the process, as this will, most likely, be your most expensive and time-consuming activity of your strategic plan. Additionally, it is important to submit that higher education (college) does not automatically equal higher wages or a fulfilling career.

"...higher education (college) does not automatically equal higher wages or a fulfilling career."

There are tons of postsecondary options that don't require a four-year degree. In some cases, a two-year degree is more than enough, and the company may even pay for the other two years of a four-year program. There's also trade school, community college, and other types of options based on the type of career you choose. This is also important to know if you are considering a career change.

Lastly, some careers or jobs only require some college. When this term is listed, do not assume anything. You should call the human resources department and ask them to define what some college means. For most jobs, there is no getting around their education requirements. However, there are instances where companies will give you experience credit in place of a portion of their education requirement. Again, call and ask the question.

Even for most entry-level jobs, the term *essential skills* will assuredly come up during an interview. Essential skills are those skills needed to operate in a high-paced and dynamic work environment. Skills such as verbal, reading, and writing skills, word-processing or typing skills, basic computer skills, etc., are a requirement for most jobs today.

There are a host of adult learning programs that focus on developing essential skills. In scenarios like this, it is terrible to see a person make no attempt to get certain types of jobs because they lack confidence in their essential skills. The essential skills gap is a major issue, as it relates to employability. However, the epidemic continues because of the stigma associated with a slow or disabled learner. Please refer to your SWOTlution™ results—and then get over it. Ask for help.

> *"...my math skills were laughable... my academic advisor recommended I take one full year of basic math before enrolling in college algebra."*

I spent years as a non-traditional student who struggled in math. I was a father of two, a husband, a pastor, and was flying six to eight hours every other day and night. However, I wanted to be an engineer. I was terrible at math and never applied myself in middle or high school. As a result, my math skills were laughable. I scored so bad on the math placement test that my academic advisor recommended I take one full year of basic math before enrolling in college algebra.

I was humbled and even a little embarrassed as I rode my bike (we only had one car) to Western Oklahoma State Community College, on Mondays, Wednesdays, and Fridays from 7 p.m. until 9:45 p.m. for forty weeks. Yep—I sat in a basic math class with around 15 advanced 8th and 9th graders who were hoping to be merit scholars. It needed to be done—so I did it. My math is better too.

Listen, it takes courage to identify a learning need or disability. It takes more courage to do something about it. For those reading this book who have a desire to break out of your laborer-type job, but are not confident in your ability, get ready! I'm asking you to humble yourself—enroll in an adult learning program that focuses on developing essential skills. These skills have been defined in various ways. However, they basically revolve around:

- Reading and writing skills
- Use of digital technology and associated software
- Adaptability
- Attitude
- Communication (verbal and written)
- Creative thinking skills
- Work ethic
- Teamwork and collaboration skills
- Networking and relationship building
- Decision-making
- Positivity
- Time management and punctuality
- Motivation
- Flexibility
- Problem-solving
- Conflict resolution
- Desire to continuously learn or to become a lifelong learner

Unfortunately, more and more companies are identifying a negative trend regarding potential candidates—they are severely lacking in essential skills. I recently worked for a group of colleges that launched a program to tackle this issue head on. It is such a concern, that several businesses actually funded the program to make it free. They even guaranteed a job interview for students who completed the essential skills program. Here's my point—there are a host of programs designed to help you achieve the appropriate skill level needed to become your vision.

I also recommend you hire a skills coach. In some cases, the work of skills coaches is grant funded. In other cases, they may just want to help. For instance, where there is a demonstrated financial need, I offer essential skills coaching and talent development for free. If you are ever in the San Antonio area, schedule an appointment at www.StrategyBrother.com. We got you.

Experience. You cannot get away from the experience requirement—it is non-negotiable. It's the tried and true data point that companies and business are truly looking for. Like the education requirement, some employers will allow candidates to substitute a certain amount of experience for education. However, just because a candidate has experience, doesn't always remove the education requirement. This why the Big Three are depicted by a triangle—all three sides are equally important.

The other strategic concept to keep in mind when conducting your research is what *type* of experience is needed. All experience is not good experience. However, sometimes you need the salary to finance getting your *other* experience. An example of this might be when a person writes their book during the day, and waits tables at night.

The table-waiting job is just to pay for the startup book-writing career. Here's another secret weapon to success—If you know the job is only about the salary, never get settled in that job. It's only a temporary sacrifice, a strategic delay. Don't even unpack your suitcase or decorate your cubicle. It will serve as a constant reminder that this is not your vision. Remember, you are doing this, just to do that. This is the Three-Move Principle at it's finest.

On the other hand, some jobs are terrible, but give you great experience. Oftentimes, you must take a job for the experience and not the pay. I learned very early on—some jobs you work just for the experience. The experience is more valuable than the wage.

I realize this is not always possible for African Americans when the generational poverty and education gaps are considered. However, it doesn't mean you cannot work for free on weekends, off days, or late nights a few days a week. Go get the experience. It will separate you from your competitors.

Many of my inexperienced clients are shocked when I make them call companies and business to offer their night or weekend labor for free. However, this is the kind of experience you just might need to get you over the top. Trust me, this works—no one will turn down free work.

This discussion reminds me a lot of my church-planting days. When we hired our general contractors, I always offered my services for free. When I say services, I mean my muscles and sweat. I helped with everything from plumbing, framing and drywall, windows, doors, floors, landscaping, to painting and trim work. I even assisted the interior decorators.

> *"...you are really working for experience, and not the money."*

I do the same thing in my neighborhood. When I see a new construction team show up for a job, I go and volunteer my services for free. If they let me, I help in the areas I want to learn in. There is unspeakable negotiating power in knowing how much a service truly cost and how much labor really goes into a project. In other cases, I have learned so much that I can do the work myself. Here's another secret weapon to success—you are really working for experience, not the money. Strategic thinkers know at some point you have to work for the experience and not the money.

To the surprise of my family and friends, I pick up new skills and experience every time. At this point, I can do just about everything, but electrical, plumbing, and concrete. If I ever needed to, I'm confident I could become a general contractor and do well for my family. *Ya gotta be desperate to learn, you must be hungry to get good experience—even during your off or down times.* I mean, how bad do you want it? Research the type of experience you need to become your vision and go get it. *Go* get it.

Certification. This is the ultimate in secret weapons. It's the part of the Big Three that often goes unnoticed and forgotten about. This—is what can take you to the next level. This—can set you apart from your peers.

This—can result in a legitimate demand for higher wages. Professional certifications are proof that you are still developing and are a lifelong learner.

Most industries have associations that serve as their professional development body. These associations help keep professionals in the loop as to industry changes and emerging trends. They ensure your skills remain relevant and sharp. This is often done through a certain number of Continuing Education Units (CEUs), Continuing Learning Units (CLUs), or some other acronym to track training and development activities.

Your research will uncover the governing body or the most popular association for the career or job you want to obtain. If there is no association, look for a similar association that offers training or certification that your industry values or unanimously recognizes.

Here are some example areas where professional certifications are offered:

- Change Management
- Project Management
- Human Resource Management
- Life and Success Coaching
- Counselor and Advising
- Certified Peer Specialist
- Safety and Mishap Prevention
- Food Safety and Food Handler
- Higher Education
- Process Improvement
- Cloud Architect

Gaining a professional certification will require both time and money. Some employers will subsidize the costs of gaining a certification if they feel it benefits the company. In other cases, it will cost you some of your personal money.

When researching what certification to get, you must be careful—nowadays everybody is offering a professional certification. However, every certification is not validated or accredited. As a matter of fact, even the term accredited doesn't mean what is used to.

A great way to determine the validity and value of a professional certification is to look at what companies are asking for on their job descriptions or job announcements. If all else fails, call the human resources department, or even consider hiring a headhunter.

Strategic Networking. The third tool best used in getting the information and gathering the facts is networking. You must network with the right people—who know the right people. It's hard to admit, but there are often cases where it really is about *who you know*. Then, there are other cases where it's about *who you get to know!* Strategic thinkers know they must be in the building, they must be at the parties, they must be at the fundraisers, and they must be at the charity golf tournaments. This is not an option. Trust. I hated it, but it was strategically necessary.

"A few drinks later, I knew them on a first name basis—I was in. Shady? Nah, this wasn't shady, this was strategic."

During my early Air Force days, I discovered the power of being at *the events*. The people who made the decisions, the people with the power, were *always* at the *events*. Here, they were freely accessible. A few drinks later, I knew them on a first name basis—I was *in*. Shady? Nah, this wasn't shady, this was strategic.

To me, this was no different than getting my hands on that rolled-up book by Bobby Fischer. It was no different than looking for food, shelter, and water after a plane crash into enemy territory. It was a reconnaissance mission. It was a chess move. I was there to gather data, to get business cards, and to make an elevator pitch if given the opportunity. Here's another secret to success—you cannot blaze a trail being anti-social. Gooo tooo the Christmas party!

This is especially difficult for African Americans. The culture shock during our strategic journeys can be mind-blowing. And before you say, "I'm not going to Planet Hollywood bruh," let me tell you a quick story.

Throughout my career I have often been the only *brother* in the building, or at the event. This was never easy. I was often peer-pressured or misunderstood, because I did not want to participate in something that *everybody* else was doing. I remember being in Moscow, Russia and everyone was excited to be there—except for me. As I normally did, I had an all-white crew. And yet again, I tried to tell them I didn't feel comfortable just walking around *freely* in foreign places. I expressed to them *we* didn't always have that luxury.

Only a few days earlier, I was kicked out of a bookstore in Stuttgart, Germany where the bookstore owner started screaming at me in German. I didn't understand a word he said, but I certainly recognized his message. I later found out he was hurling racial slurs at me and telling me to get out of his store. My crew laughingly apologized for the incident and just *kept it moving*. I was furious.

> *"...please don't tell me you can't stomach going to a wine and cheese social, or to have a lunch meeting at the local Hooters."*

So now, here in Russia, my crew finally conceited and said, "Okay, we will just see you later then." I decided I would stay in the 5-star hotel and just eat there. Nope—they wouldn't serve me. I decided to bolt for McDonald's, just a few blocks away. I walked with my head straight and was minding my business when a Russian police officer started harassing me. Once again, I knew the message. Get back to the hotel, now!

I sat in the lobby and *angry-cried* until my crew returned with Russian mementos, t-shirts, and had been obviously drinking. I told them what happened and one of them went to the McDonald's to get me something to eat. This went on for two more days, and countless times in France,

STRATEGIC PLANNING

Turkey, Belgium, and to many more places to name here. So, please don't tell me you can't stomach going to a wine and cheese social, or to have a lunch meeting at the local Hooters.

In order to get the information and to gather the facts, you must be willing to deal with the *majority* culture of your chosen industry or sector. Remember, this is our 21st century civil rights movement. You must blaze a trail for others to follow, then expose and restructure that system. You've heard it before, and I'm going to say it again—you *gotta* play the game! Stay focused. Your grandchildren's success may very well depend on it.

You see, I needed that Russia and Germany mission to get nominated for an annual award later that year. I needed to be on that trip, I needed that *shine* to get the award I was seeking. I knew winning that award would set me apart from my peers. It was an **opportunity**—remember your SWOT. Only one enlisted person was selected for those kinds of missions.

I needed that award to make me competitive for a job that was known for helping enlisted men and women get commissioned to the officer ranks. Yep, I was using the Three-Move Principle™. This trip was strategic, and so was the sacrifice—too easy.

A year later, I got the job I planned for. Three years later, I received a direct commission as the USAF's first African American man to be selected as an aerospace physiologist. You see—the Russians and the Germans had something I needed. Thank you Germany, thank you Russia—*Got 'em.*

My stepdad and his friend also had something I needed, a secret weapon they hid from me for years. And when I got my hands on it, I quickly closed the skill gap. I learned a valuable lesson that summer. In order to be great at something, you must be willing to study—you must do your *homework*. This makes sense, especially for a strategic game like chess. No wonder more chess books have been written than books about all other sports and games combined!

Like that summer in the *rug store,* life information is sometimes rolled-up in somebody's back pocket. Yes, it may be hard to find, but it's out there. You just have to be at the event, in the building, or on the mission.

Don't stop until you find it. When you find it, you will discover what it's going take to achieve your goals. And just like those OGs taught me that summer, "Don't ever wait on somebody to give you the information—go get it yourself."

Speaking of that summer, I never saw *Rug-Man* again, nor did I ever go back to the *rug store*. A few months later, the cops raided our house—my stepfather went to jail for a while this time, and I changed schools yet again. This made five schools in six years. I was heartbroken, depressed, and suddenly in a predominately white school. Me, my mother, and my little brother needed a strategy—big time!

I never played chess again until 2019—the year I wrote this book. As a matter of fact, it wasn't until I finished writing this chapter that I realized it. As a result, I dedicate my first game, since 1989, to the men who taught me to look in every man's back pocket before shaking his hand. My first move is in honor of the OGs—the original strategic thinkers.

It's Your Move

Ultimately, your research results will provide you with what it takes to achieve your vision. Remember, there are three big areas you must maximize if you want to break through the glass ceiling—education, experience, and certification. Now it's time to get to work. In the space provided below, please write the necessary requirements needed to become your vision. Be sure to consider what you want to be paid. Remember, your salary will be commensurate with your education and experience levels, and the types of certification you hold.

Education Requirements

In order to become my vision, I need to obtain the following educational requirements:

_____
_____
_____

Experience Requirements

In order to become my vision, I need this type and amount of experience:

_____
_____
_____

Certification Requirements

In order to become my vision, I need to obtain the following professional certifications:

_____
_____
_____

Let's Play: Openings

Now that you know the pieces and the board, it's time to begin. The first moves of a chess game are called the *opening* or *opening moves*. The first move may seem simple and insignificant, but it's not. Remember, every move and every piece counts. According to Wheeler (2019), "Your opening move will provide better protection of the King, control over an area of the board (particularly the center), greater mobility for pieces, and possibly opportunities to capture opposing pawns and pieces."[xxxv]

The opening moves or sequences have names and have been studied by chess experts for hundreds of years, maybe even thousands if you go back to 550 A.D. in northwest India.

The possible opening moves of chess have been extensively studied for hundreds of years, and many of these sequences have been given names to simplify discussion of the game. It is fascinating to think that your first move can have such a huge impact on the rest of your game. I will briefly list a few of the most common opening moves to help you get started. I recommend you go to the hundreds of chess how-to websites to truly grasp each of the following openings.

Ruy Lopez. Named after the 16th century Spanish clergyman and chess enthusiast—also called the "Spanish" opening—starts out as:

1. e4, e5

2. Nf3, Nc6

3. Bb5

Giuoco Piano. First developed in the 1600s and perhaps the oldest chess opening, the Giuoco Piano is a popular chess opening from the beginner levels all the way up to experts. Giuoco Piano translates from Italian into the «quiet game». It starts as:

1. e4, e5

2. Nf3, Nc6

3. Bc4, Bc5

Sicilian Defense (for black pieces). The Sicilian is very popular among chess experts. As a matter of fact, "Almost one-quarter of all games use the Sicilian Defense."[xxxvi] Wheeler states, "Black immediately fights for the center, but by attacking from the c-file (instead of mirroring White's move) he creates an asymmetrical position that leads to lots of complicated positions." The Sicilian Defense starts as:

1. e4, c5

French Defense (for black pieces). In the French Defense, Black lets White have more control over the center, in exchange for which he builds a hopefully safe wall of pawns. The French Defense starts as:

1. e4, e6

2. d4, d5

The list of opening moves could go on for pages. I have listed a few of the easier openings just so you could understand that the opening move is not just an opening move—it's strategic. For further study, here is a list of additional openings.[xxxvii]

- Caro-Kann Defense
- Pirc Defense
- Queen's Gambit
- Indian Defenses
- English Opening
- Reti Opening

DEVELOPING YOUR SUCCESS MAP

Chess great Bobby Fischer did something amazing in that book. He laid out how you were going to play, before you started playing. He forced you to visualize it before you did it—he empowered you with a vision! He called it "programmed instruction." Programmed instruction is a method of presenting new subject matters to students in a graded sequence of controlled steps. Yes, small and controlled, spelled out steps. This is what made this book so instrumental to my chess game—to my life.

In his book, Mr. Fischer presented a visual illustration for new chess players, and you know what? He was on to something. Approximately 65 percent of the population are visual learners.[xxxviii] This means more than half of us learn through pictures, graphs, and illustrations. Drawing your picture, creating a map, and painting your vision may be the most important step of the strategic planning process. This picture is your Success Map™.

Preparing for your Success Map. This Success Map will be your masterpiece, your atlas, and your playbook. To others, it will look like a bunch of arrows, triangles, squares, circles, erased and rewritten goals, barely readable notes, and brown rings from your sweating coffee mug. It might be taped to the wall in your living room, glued to the ceiling in your bedroom, or the wallpaper on your phone. It will be the document you check after each move—ensuring you are still on track. It's your GPS. You will look at it time and time again—staring at it like Fischer and his chessboard.

After you've unearthed the whispered generational secrets, after you have read every rolled-up book and have collected all your data—you must now brainstorm and develop your success map. First, you need to find a private workspace or room with large work surfaces, chalkboards, whiteboards, smart boards, etc. Or, you can purchase butcher paper and masking tape and create writing surfaces wherever you can. If need be, just take it to the kitchen table—but you already know, momma *ain't* having that for too long.

Put all your data in one place. Now, you must put all your research in one single place. It's okay if it looks like a huge mess—your goal was to collect and gather as much data as possible. The more information you have, the better.

Categorize the Data. To put it in perspective, imagine you have a jar filled with the data you collected from your research. You carefully dump the data onto a large table in the center of the room—you must now patiently categorize it. You need to put things in categories that make sense to you.

The depiction below is an illustration of how I recommend you categorize your data. In the jar on the left you have:

1. Circles—Represent your **Education Data**. What kind of education or training do you need to become your vision?

2. Xs—Represent your **Experience Data.** What kind and how much experience do you need to become your vision?

3. Squares—Represent your **Certification Data**. What type of professional certification do you need to become your vision? How you can get ahead of your peers?

You must put all the information in the correct categories as depicted on the right. These are now your **Data Groups**.

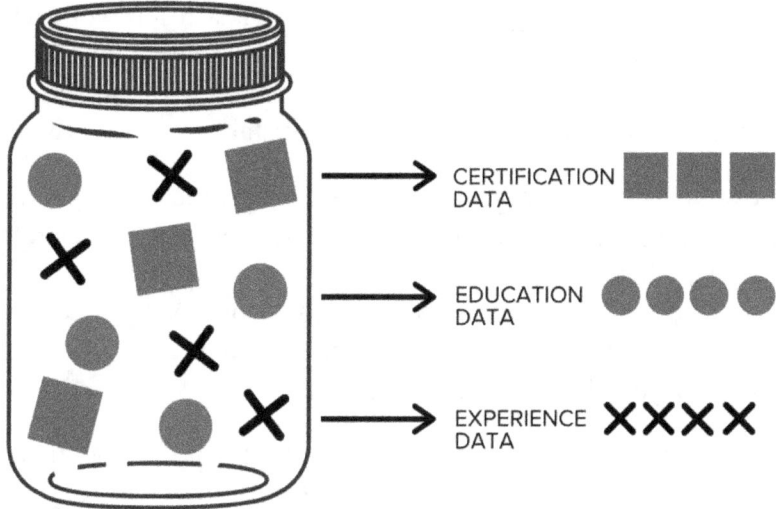

Now that you have data groups, you will organize them into a step chart:

1. What you must do first? Example—Step 1, Step 2, Step 3…

    a. Always put the step that's going to take the longest as Step 1— this will be your Critical Step (more on your Critical Step later).

2. What you will do last?

3. What you can do at the same time?

    a. During the same step and simultaneously.

4. Determine how long it will take to become your vision.

5. Determine how many steps it will take.

6. Determine how many activities you will have to accomplish.

Your Critical Step is the longest and the non-negotiable activity in your step chart. Critical Step errors are major—limit them or they might derail your timetable. You cannot afford to make careless errors and bad decisions regarding your Critical Step.

For example, let's say you need to get five years of experience as a store manager to qualify for the regional manager job. Your Critical Step is five years. This means your other steps are less than five years and are not mandatory for the regional manager job. As a result, you cannot afford to get fired from your current job as a store manager. It will be difficult to get another job as a store manager to get the five years of experience you need. This is a Critical Step mistake.

Other examples might be getting the necessary experience you need to qualify for a promotion or getting your graduate degree. Therefore, skipping class, being constantly late to work, missing deadlines, doing poor work, spending more time on breaks or on your phone are all examples of things I've seen destroy someone's strategic plan. Your Critical Step is just that—Critical! Don't blow it.

You can also put two or more activities in one step if they can be done at the same time. Here is another secret weapon to success—strategic thinkers are experts at multi-tasking and compartmentalization. In my opinion, these two skills are the most important strategic planning skills.

In the bottom row of your step chart, you now have how many steps it will take, how long, and how many activities you will have to do to become your vision.

Here is an example of a step chart populated with our previously collected and categorized data:

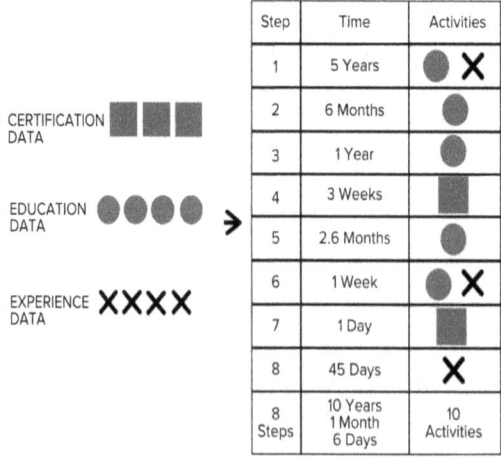

Congratulations! Your data is now organized and in a clean format. Now comes the fun part, it's time to create you Success Map! Your Success Map should be easy to read by someone else, especially your thought-partners or potential funders. The Success Map will provide you your first glimpse of your strategic process. Think of your Success Map as a snapshot or picture of your strategic plan. In other words, if your strategic plan took a *selfie*—it would look like the Success Map. Your Success Map makes it easy for you and others to quickly see:

- What you are doing
- Achievements and victories
- How long it will take for you to reach your goal and vision
- If you are on schedule
- What you have left to do
- Where you may need help
- And more

The Success Map will eventually become part of a formal book report style strategic plan. Keep in mind that the level and type of strategic plan you produce will be based on your industry sector. If your vision is to launch an urgent care clinic or some other business, a Success Map will be very high-level with few details. This will become part of your business plan. Business planning is a subset of strategic planning. Therefore, one of your steps will be to create a business plan. A business plan is different from a strategic plan in that it focuses on a more short-term perspective and will include information like fundraising and potential funding streams, risk analyses, projected budget and profit potential, a market analysis, a list of associates or business partners, etc. It is normal for lenders, investors, directors, and potential business partners to ask for a copy of your business plan.

This book focuses on strategic planning for you as an individual and not on your company or organization. If you plan on launching a business, you will need to take your strategic plan and use it to create a business plan. If this is you—hopefully, you developed your strategic plan with your business vision in mind. If not, start over and align your vision with your work accordingly. Creating your Success Map will do wonders for both you and your business plan.

There are many ways and styles to create a Success Map—there is no right or wrong way. I recommend you keep it simple and easy to read. Most software programs (e.g., PowerPoint©) have *smart art* or pre-developed shapes you can use to create a Success Map. I recommend using the simplest format possible. The Success Map should not be overly complicated.

See the illustration on the next page. This is the format my clients and I use when creating their Success Maps. This map (The Playbook™) is formatted to fit the pages of this book. To get a full sized version, subscribe to www.strategybrother.com

VISION: Become the State's Top 3rd Grade Educator.
MISSION: Implement Education Equity Programs for At-Risk 3rd Graders.

Step 1: Earn B.S. Elementary Education

Activity 1: Maintain 3.5 GPA

Activity 2: Volunteer at Local Schools

Activity 3: Apply for and complete a K - 6 Internship

Activity 4: Summer of junior year start applying for jobs in at-risk areas or school districts

Activity 5: Network! Spend four years attending every developmental and education advocacy event available

Step 2: Complete State Approved Educator Prep Program (EPP)

Activity 1: Register for an EPP that will work with my current volunteer schedule

Activity 2: Use the opportunity to network with the administrators and fellow classmates

Activity 3: Look for on-the-job opportunities at the EPP location

Activity 4: Keep applying for jobs in at-risk areas or school districts

Step 3: Pass the Certification Exams

Activity 1: Register for exam

Activity 2: Study to polish skills

Activity 3: Keep applying for jobs in at-risk areas or school districts (until I get a job)

Activity 4: Submit applications for official teacher certification after passing exam

Step 4: Begin Teaching 3rd Grade

Activity 1: Engage parents immediately

Activity 2: Network with the administrators and fellow classmates

Activity 3: Compete for annual awards at school, district, regional, and state levels

Figure 11.1, The Playbook™

STRATEGIC PLANNING

VISION:_____
MISSION:_____

MONITOR PROGRESS

Step 1:

Activity 1:
Activity 2:
Activity 3:
Activity 4:
Activity 5:

Step 2:

Activity 1:
Activity 2:
Activity 3:
Activity 4:
Activity 5:

MONITOR PROGRESS

Step 3:

Activity 1:
Activity 2:
Activity 3:
Activity 4:
Activity 5:

Step 4:

Activity 1:
Activity 2:
Activity 3:
Activity 4:
Activity 5:

MONITOR PROGRESS

Figure 11.2, The Playbook™

It's Your Move

Answer the following:

1. Drawing your picture, creating a snapshot, and painting your vision may be the most important step of the strategic planning process. This picture is called your _____.

2. T/F You must categorize your data and then number it in a way that identifies what you must do first and what will be done last.

3. The _____ is the item that will determine how long it will take for you to reach your goal.

4. If your strategic plan took a *selfie*, it would look like the Success Map. Your Success Map makes it easy for you and others to quickly see:

    - _____
    - _____
    - _____
    - _____
    - _____
    - _____
    - And more

STRATEGIC PLANNING

Let's Play: Decision-Making During the Game

Your chess skills can be improved with practice. The more you play, the better you get. Additionally, the more games you play, the more opportunity you get to develop your own personal strategy. Part of your game strategy is how you make decisions during the game. World Grandmaster, Raluca Sgîrcea[xxxix], lists five things to consider when making real-time decisions. Mastering these strategies will not happen overnight, but will become second nature with practice. Here are Sgîrcea's five suggested steps:

1. Identify your opponent's threat

It should become a reflex for you to ask yourself, what does my opponent want to do with his last move? It doesn't have to be a deadly threat that you are looking for all the time. It could be an idea, a plan he'd like to achieve.

Why is it helpful to do this? Besides lowering the risk of hanging a piece or blundering material, you can discover hidden prophylactic moves that put your opponent's ideas on hold. Remember – it's important to find a good plan, but it is equally important to keep your opponent from improving his own position.

2. Identify the weaknesses

This step should be applied for both your opponent's position and yours. In order to find a suitable plan, you first need to know what you are playing for. Look at your opponent's position and find its weaknesses – it could be a weak pawn, square, but also a badly placed piece or an open king.

At the same time, you have to be aware that your opponent is probably doing the same–scanning your position. Identify your own weaknesses and look for ways to get rid of them or strive for positions where your opponent can't use them in his favor.

3. Improve your pieces

The next thing on your list should be to look for your worst placed pieces. By this, we mean pieces that have no real use so far in the position and can be improved. Look for better, more active squares, but at the same time, safe for them. Then, try to find a way to reach them.

If it's not too complicated, won't take too long, and your opponent cannot easily stop you, then you've got yourself an interesting idea to achieve.

4. Play against your opponent's pieces

The same way you did with your own pieces, do this with your opponent's. Identify their worst placed pieces and prevent them from getting active by reaching better squares.

Pay attention to exchanges as well – trade with the rival's most active pieces and try to leave him with your bad ones.

5. Identify your advantage

If you haven't gotten an answer to your position so far, you can do one more thing – think on which side of the board you have an advantage. It could be more active pieces or pressure on a certain file or initiative. That is usually the side of the board you must take action on.

These steps should help you identify the correct move and plan in most of the positions. You don't have to come up with an answer for each one of them – it could be only one of them that contains the answer to your position.

As you can see, the decision-making process in chess is eerily similar to the decision-making process in life. When Sgîrcea's five suggested steps are applied to personal or professional strategic planning, it becomes apparent why chess is used to teach people to think strategically. Actually, these five steps offer a great snapshot of general strategic planning. Now that you are a strategic thinker, this chess advice will resonate with you in a way that it might not have before reading this book.

CHAPTER TWELVE

WARNING: NO DISCIPLINE—NO DESTINY

From a young age, chess players are conditioned to build stamina for prolonged thought (Melekhina, 2015). This stamina proves priceless when chess games extend into the third or fourth hour. Many chess players are really good when it's a short game. However, the *real-ones* are separated from the pretenders when the game goes long. This is because it requires an unbelievable level of discipline to stay focused for such a long time. By the way, the longest chess game in history was in 1989 and was 20 hours and fifteen minutes!

You cannot become great at chess, follow a success map, live out your core values, make good decisions, or restructure systems of inequity without discipline. That Success Map you just created is just a blank piece of paper if you don't have discipline. Discipline is defined as "training to act in accordance with rules" (Webster, 2019). Following the rules or a set of pre-determined steps for extended periods of time is not always easy.

In chess, discipline is non-negotiable. Discipline is also non-negotiable for strategic thinkers.

"A strategic thinker with no discipline is just full of hot–air and will eventually be exposed."

STRATEGIC PLANNING 111

Strategic thinkers can follow a strategic plan, because they have discipline. A strategic thinker with no discipline is just full of hot-air and will eventually be exposed. These types of people are always talking, but rarely follow up with measurable achievements. Don't be that person.

Aimless talk and idle words are time wasters and rank with fabrication—every strategic thinker knows this. My momma used to tell me, "somebody talking too much is lying about something" (Crawford, 1988). Additionally, my wife, Erika, always reminds me to talk less. She's a firm believer that people who talk too much give away their secrets. They unknowingly forfeit their intellectual property—research the history of Jack Daniel's whiskey. She's right. Someone is always waiting to rob your ideas. Let your game speak for itself. Please be quiet. Please be disciplined.

> *"...when discipline's required, people tend to quit. Don't be a quitter, have some discipline."*

A few months ago, I was watching an interview of Laker-great, Kobe Bryant. As an avid Spurs fan, I have no love lost for Mr. Bryant. However, I was amazed as Kobe described his level of daily commitment and work habits. I began to wonder, *Was it his work or his talent that made him great?* While I believe it was a little of both, I also believe he would be just another really good two-guard if he didn't have that killer instinct—that discipline. Instead, he was a great two-guard, one of the greatest.

Unfortunately, this is the area where many people fail. They simply lack the discipline to stick to the plan—to follow through. For instance, if you have only skimmed through this book, you have missed many key points. Resultantly, when you try to put your plan together, you will be utterly clueless and may even give up. It's not too late, go back and re-read the parts you hurried through. Remember, every move counts and this game will go on the rest of your life. Here's another secret weapon to success—when discipline's required, people tend to quit. Don't be a quitter, have some discipline.

As a strategic thinker, you should pray the promotion you're competing for requires high levels of hard work and discipline. You will have the advantage. I taught my children this regarding their collegiate track and field careers. I forced them to understand that talented people have great track meets, but committed people have great track careers.

Just before his freshman year at North Carolina State University, I shared with my son, Dorian Jr., that life would defeat people off the track that he'd never defeat on the track. Relationship drama, money, sex and unexpected pregnancies, grades, drugs, alcohol, etc., would destroy his competitors with no discipline. I can speak to this—I was that competitor with no discipline. Very simply put, it's attrition. Attrition is the unfortunate truth that everybody who starts, won't finish. Attrition is an advantage for strategic thinkers. This may seem harsh to some, but not to strategic thinkers. Get over it. You better prepare your kids for the real world, ASAP!

If you teach your children, the Three-Move Principle™ early, they'll advance well ahead of their peers. Additionally, you must empower them with success maps and strategies that align with your family's core values. Be intentional about disciplining them in the area of strategic thinking—it will pay off later.

For instance, I intentionally trained and guided my children to run the hurdles in track and field. I did this because the hurdles are hard—and you know what happens to people when things get hard. We taught them from the beginning—pain and fear can, and will, neutralize talent. Running the hurdles is about more than speed. The hurdles require hundreds of other additional factors that require high levels of discipline. Bring it.

"...championships and school records are good—careers, salaries, bonuses, community and kingdom service are better."

This truth significantly increased their chances of success—victory though attrition is real. My children knew they might not be the fastest off the backside of the hurdles or have the best start, but they could make up for it by being the most consistent, the most disciplined, have the best diet, have the least amount of fear, etc. My point is, don't be afraid to strive for what seems difficult. Here's another secret weapon to success—the degree of difficulty doesn't decrease your chances of success, it actually increases it. Remember, people with little discipline quit when things become difficult. You have the advantage!

Strategically speaking, it was never just about track and field. Track was simply the mechanism we used—it was the tool available to us. You too must use the tools available to you. God gifted you with something, a talent or skill that you do better than everyone else. For my family, it's our athleticism. However, we taught our children that running is what they do, not who they are. National championships and school records are good, but careers, salaries, bonuses, and community and kingdom service are better.

Yes, the person applying for the promotion may be better at some things than you are, but remember to embrace your strengths and identify your weaknesses. As a strategic thinker, you have more discipline! I repeat, some achievements require more discipline than talent—this is your advantage! Below are a few indicators of people with little-to-no discipline:

- They have punctuality issues and are rarely on time.
- They struggle to finish tasks.
- They don't *walk it like they talk it.*
- They put things off to the last minute and procrastinate.
- They get easily distracted.
- They have no life goals and aren't interested in developing any.
- They are impulsive—especially with money.

Unfortunately, there are not enough pages in this book to discuss why some people will struggle to follow through or might never commit to self-improvement. As a result, I believe it's more beneficial to discuss how to prevent these threats to success. Here are ten ways to develop better discipline:

1. Don't try to do too many activities at one time.
2. Celebrate smaller victories like they are larger victories.
3. Schedule frequent breaks and recovery time.
4. Hire or enlist a mentor or life coach to hold you accountable.
5. Don't put anything off for longer than one-hour—anything!
6. Honor your scheduled "development time" appointments.
7. With your mentor/coach, revisit your core values, vision, and mission monthly or more where needed.
8. Follow your strategic plan exactly how you created it—revise where necessary.
9. Be optimistic and positive. Feed yourself with positive declarations and words of affirmation.
10. Surround yourself with consistent winners and distance yourself from consistent losers. **Note:** This is often the most difficult step. It can be divisive or even alienate the people you love the most. However, you are not creating a lifetime of distance. You're only creating enough space for you to achieve your goals without pessimism. Once you master your technique, go back and teach them how you did it. *Haters gon' hate tho*—so be ready.

The fact is, no matter how hard we try, we are all going to occasionally come up short. And guess what? We should. Here's another secret to success—if you haven't failed yet, you are failing! This suggests your visions and goals have never been bold enough. It's been too easy, too small, and with too little impact. I know as African Americans we are sometimes risk averse and for good reason, but you cannot innovate or create where there is a prohibition of failure. *Shoot your shot!*

We fail sometimes—it's okay. However, you must be disciplined enough to have a short recovery time. You must be quick to forgive yourself. I have learned one of the most valuable traits exhibited by strategic thinkers is how quick they forgive, starting with themselves. You cannot make the chess move of your life holding grudges—especially against yourself. Own what you need to own and keep it moving.

Every chess player knows they'll lose at some point. However, the key is to learn from mistakes and develop corrective measures. This takes discipline. Discipline can be learned, but it takes practice to stay disciplined. Guess what? Most people don't like to practice—checkmate!

As a strategic thinker, you must crave scenarios that require discipline. But unfortunately, if you are the one with no discipline, there are strategic thinkers watching your every move. And like Bobby Fischer, they can go on for hours—days if need be. Got discipline?

It's Your Move

Answer the following:

1. The longest chess game in history, in 1989, was:

    a. 20 hours and fifteen minutes.

    b. 10 hours and 10 minutes

    c. 15 hours and 20 minutes

    d. 25 hours and fifteen minutes

2. T/F Good discipline is non-negotiable as a strategic thinker.

3. Below are a few indicators of people with little-to-no discipline:

    - They have punctuality issues and are rarely on time.
    - They struggle to finish tasks.
    - They don't *walk it like they talk it*.
    - They put things off to the last minute and procrastinate.
    - They get easily distracted.
    - They don't know what they want to be.

- They don't know what they want to do with their lives.

4. T/F   People cannot innovate or create where there is a prohibition of failure.

5. T/F   As a strategic thinker, you must crave scenarios that require discipline.

Let's Play: Special Moves[xl]

Pawn Promotion. Pawns are the weakest pieces on the board, but they have the potential to become much stronger. Should a pawn manage to make it all the way to the other end of the board, that pawn must be promoted to any piece its player chooses, other than a king.

Generally, you would promote a pawn to a queen. However, you can also promote it to a rook, knight, or bishop. When the pawn is promoted to a queen, the move is often termed *queening*, and it is allowable for there to be two queens of the same color on the board. Sometimes a rook is used in an inverted position to designate the second queen.

Promoting to something other than a queen is known as *underpromotion*. Since the queen is the most powerful piece, *promotion* is only for a queen. However, there may be a rare instance where the movement of a knight or other piece might offer an immediate benefit, in which case underpromotion is used.

En Passant. *En passant*—a French term that means "in passing"—is probably the most confusing move for novice chess players. Players may not even know the move exists, making it the source of many arguments.

Before the 15th century, most people played by rules that didn't allow pawns to move two squares on their first move. When the two-square-pawn move was added to speed up the opening phase of the game, players noticed that the pawn could now sneak by an enemy pawn—something that was never possible when pawns plodded along at one square per move.

The solution was *en passant*, a move that allows a pawn that has moved two squares to be captured as though it had only moved one.

The following conditions must all be present for an *en passant* capture to be legal:

- The capturing pawn must be on its fifth rank.

- The opponent must move a pawn two squares, landing the pawn directly alongside the capturing pawn on the fifth rank.

- You must make the capture immediately. You only get one chance to capture *en passant*.

- If all those conditions are met, an *en passant* capture is possible.

In our next "Let's Play" segment we will cover winning the game—check and checkmate.

CHAPTER THIRTEEN

HOW ARE YOU DOING?
EVALUATING YOUR PROGRESS

In chess, constant board observation is a must. Watching every move and knowing every position on the chessboard is how you monitor game progression. In other words, you must *babysit* the board, if you don't—you'll get behind. It's no different than losing points you don't call when playing dominoes or receiving a negative score for underbidding your potential books in spades. In the two examples above, you lose something for not paying attention—in chess, you lose board awareness.

Board awareness empowers you with real-time feedback on how you are doing in the game. I personally do an intentional 15-second awareness check before and after each of my moves, and again after each of my opponent's moves. Every chess player has their own way of maintaining board awareness. As a novice, I frame my awareness checks around my strategy of controlling the center of the board. You will do the same type of monitoring regarding your strategic plan.

While executing your strategic plan, you must monitor and assess your progress. You must evaluate your performance and answer one important question, "How am I doing?" This step of the process is the key to you becoming your vision. A clearly defined evaluation process will increase your probability of success. Likewise, a biased and poorly defined evaluation process will cost you time and money. It is impossible to be strategic, without an honest look at how you are performing.

However, there is a major problem that can plague us all. We *cain't* always be told *nothing*! Let me be clear in stating, it is my opinion that very few people graciously welcome constructive criticism. I found this particularly difficult. However, I stubbornly and begrudgingly realized, I needed help. I needed a trusted agent or thought-partner to tell me when I was veering off course and was not following the plan as designed. I needed a mentor who was where I was trying to get—and so do you.

It will save you time and money to have somebody hold you accountable as you work through the activities of your Success Map. Remember, asking for help is a strategic move and not a sign of weakness. Here's another secret weapon to success—surround yourself with *Godly people* who have more and know more than you do. But, that's not enough. You must also grant them authority to speak into your life, empower them to monitor your progress, and make them part of your evaluation process. By the way, all *churchgoers* are not *godly*—be careful.

Keep your strategic objectives in mind. Keeping your previously established goals and vision in mind is key to an effective evaluation strategy. Here is where you and your mentor will refer to your SWOTlution™, core values, mission, equity challenges or issues, and Success Map steps and activities. At this point, all your data will be in a formal strategic plan and easy to find. **Note:** You will be creating your formal strategic plan at the end of this book.

Establish an assessment or coaching method. In most cases, your mentor or coach will already have a coaching method/technique. Much of this depends on the type of coach you hire. This decision should be driven by your SWOTlution™ results. In other words, which areas did you need help or further development in?

It will do you no good to hire a career coach if you need spiritual, personal, or life coaching. The same is true if you hire a skills coach, but your essential skills are above average.

You must be strategic when you hire a coach or enlist a mentor. It is imperative you hire the right person with the right methods, experience, and techniques to help you become your vision. Yes, hire! Stop expecting people to give you something for free or at a discounted rate. Please staahhp—it's a bad look on all of *us*.

Here's another secret to success—strategic thinkers spare no expense when investing in themselves. Hiring a coach is not investing in them, it's investing in you.

There are many types of coaches. Here a few examples:

⇒ Skills Coaches

⇒ Career Coaches

⇒ Personal or Life Coaches

- o Warning: Be careful about hiring a coach when you really need a licensed professional counselor or therapist. Seek guidance from your primary medical doctor.

⇒ Executive Coaches

⇒ Spiritual Coaches or Clergy

⇒ A Combo Coach (all or some combination of the above)

Regardless of the type of coach or expert you hire, a good coach should provide you with at least the Three C's:

1. **Coaching** - Help you improve or sustain.

2. **Change** - Help you revise or restructure your Success Map or refine your research data to suit emerging or shifting trends.

3. **Continue** - Help you see the finish line and identify potential threats or roadblocks. Basically, they should be able to get you to checkmate!

Schedule your evaluation sessions. Now, you must determine your evaluation frequency. In other words, how often are you and your mentor going to formally evaluate your progress? I recommend you accomplish a formal evaluation at least four times for each Success Map. Simply divide the Success Map or strategic plan into four equal sections or phases. Here is an example evaluation strategy for a Success Map with four steps and 23 activities:

Evaluation Strategy for Mr. John Q. Client

1. **Jan 6, 2020 (8 a.m.) at the coffee shop on Ackerman Road.**

    ⇒ Phase 1 Evaluation Session: Review Step 1, Activities 1 thru 5

2. **Feb 17, 2020 (1 p.m.) at the San Antonio African American Museum**

    ⇒ Phase 2 Evaluation Session: Review Step 2, Activities 6 thru 11

3. **Mar 21, 2020 (noon) at the taco shop on Farm Road 78**

    ⇒ Phase 3 Evaluation Session: Review Step 3, Activities 12 thru 18

4. **Nov 1, 2020 (10 a.m.) at Williams Consulting Group**

    ⇒ Phase 4 Evaluation Session: Review Step 4, Activities 19 - 23

    o Schedule a celebration event at the last meeting

Don't be afraid to monitor your progress. A good, honest evaluation is quite possibly the most important part of the strategic planning process. On the other hand, an incorrect or biased evaluation will all, but ensure your failure. In chess, when evaluating the board, it's not just to determine position. It's also to predict your next three moves. When evaluating your progress, you are also watching for upcoming events, unexpected threats, new opportunities, or entry points. In other words, you must always watch the board.

Be prepared to make revisions. There is a time in every chess game when you are you are hit with a surprise. Maybe your opponent is better than you thought, their opening move is not what you expected, or the board is positioned in a way you've never seen before. Regardless of the surprise, it can have a negative effect on your game strategy—unless you're prepared for it.

In every chess game, some part of your strategy will not work. The same is true for your strategic plan. If you and your mentor realize something is not working, you must find the best solution and implement it quickly. Do not allow revisions or changes to discourage you—revisions are a necessary part of the strategic planning process. A revision can be particularly discouraging when it costs you time or forces you to have to redo something or start over. Relax, this is expected.

Regardless of how it makes you feel, you cannot ignore a part of your plan that's not working or is underperforming. Things you ignore now, you will regret later. Remember, no one develops a perfect strategic plan. Even the best strategic thinkers must revise what seemed like a perfect plan. If it's broken, fix it quickly and keep it moving. If it's not broken, you're not looking hard enough.

Something unexpected or difficult will certainly happen such as loss of life, the loss of a job, legal trouble, family problems or drama, etc. These types of things are not unique to you, and can happen to anyone. However, I believe these setbacks can be opportunities to rebuild—chances to accomplish something better the second or third time around.

I'm unashamed in stating, I believe "God causes all things to work out for the good of them who love Him and who are called according to His purpose" (Romans 8:28, NASB). This verse empowers me with hope. Even when tough times arrive, I know I'm going to be all right—you will, too.

I also believe we, everyone, can do better accepting the consequences of our bad decisions. Please do not blame God, your strategic plan, or somebody else, when your bad choices caused the problem.

When thinking strategically, statements like the following make no sense at all:

- "I can't *believe* I lost my scholarship" (even though you never went to class and partied all night)
- "I can't *believe* I got her pregnant" (even though you had sex)

- "I can't *believe* I got pregnant" (even though you had sex)
- "I can't *believe*_____" (fill in the blank)

If you really think about it—you can believe it. When we fail to prevent the problem, the problem will prevent us. This is where most people quit, please don't! When something happens that threatens to derail your progress, identify how the problem affects your plan, make the necessary revisions, and get back on track. Where necessary, seek forgiveness and repent—Amen.

It's Your Move

Answer the following:

1. While executing your strategic plan, you must _____ and _____ your progress.

2. You must _____ your performance and answer one important question, "How am I doing?"

3. T/F   Keeping your previously established goals and vision in mind is key to an effective evaluation strategy.

4. T/F   You must be strategic when you hire a coach or enlist a mentor. It is imperative you hire the right person with the right methods, experience, and techniques to help you become your vision.

5. T/F   When evaluating your progress, you are also watching for upcoming events, unexpected threats, new opportunities or entry points.

6. T/F   If you and your mentor realize something is not working, you must find the best solution and implement it quickly.

Let's Play: "Check" and "Checkmate"

Check is a term that simply means a player's king is being attacked. When the King is in check, the player *must* find a way to stop the threat; it cannot be ignored. In the diagram below, the white Bishop has put the black King in check.

When a King is in check, there are three options: Black can (1) capture the checking piece (2) block the line of fire, or (3) move the King from the line of fire.[xli] In the diagram, black can use all three of these options (noted by the arrows) to remove the King from danger. There are some special cases. When in check by a Knight, there is no blocking option.

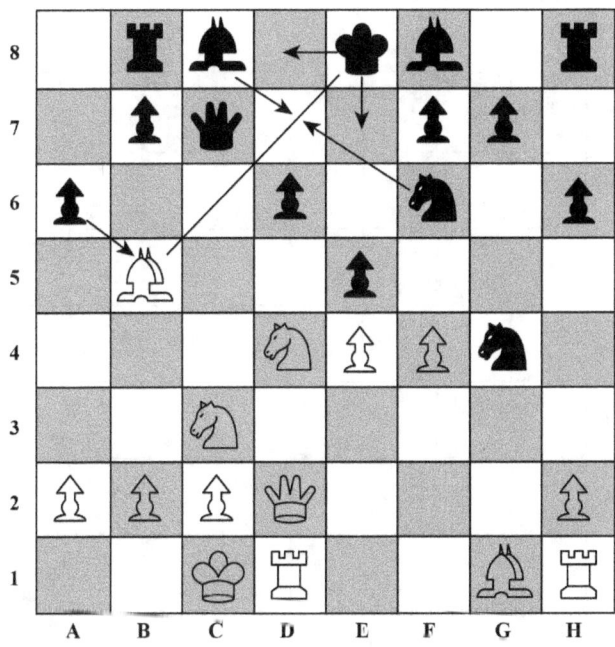

In summary, the player must do one of these things when in check:[xlii, xliii, xliv]

- *Capture* the checking piece with the King or another piece.
- *Interpose*: put a piece between the checking piece and the King. This only works if the checking piece is a long distance piece (bishop, rook, or queen).
- *Move* the King to a square which is not threatened.

If it is not possible to get the King out of check with one of the three above options, then it is called "checkmate," or simply "mate." In the diagram below is an example of checkmate. Checkmate can be accomplished by any piece on the board except for the opposing King. Checkmate (often called mate) is when a player's king is attacked (in check) and there is no way to escape that attack. Or, simply put, the King is under attack and cannot get out of being captured. Giving checkmate is the main goal in chess: a player who is mated loses the game.

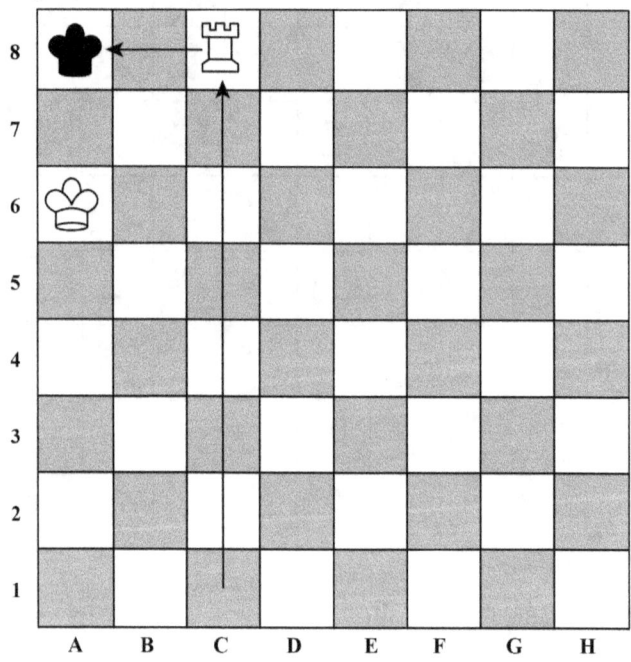

In games featuring one or two beginners, more errors are made, so many of these games end in checkmate.[xlv] Checkmates are rare in games between advanced players, because many players respectfully resign before forcing the opponent to play until the King is checkmated. An unwinnable game ends in a *stalemate*. A game will also end in a stalemate when:

- There are not enough pieces on the board to force a checkmate.

- The same exact position is repeated three times (though not necessarily three times in a row).

- Fifty consecutive moves have been played where neither player has moved a pawn or captured a piece.

In our next "Let's Play" segment, we will cover some common chess strategies.

STRATEGIC PLANNING

CHAPTER FOURTEEN

CHECKMATE! NOW WHAT?

"...you play to win the game. Hello? You don't just play to play it!" (Edwards, 2002).[xlvi] These are now infamous words from former Jets coach, Herm Edwards, during a 2002 postgame press conference. Coach Edwards became perturbed when a reporter insinuated his team might be quitting. His passionate reaction provided a sound bite that now has its own anniversary. Coach Edwards' rant provides the perfect undertone for why I wrote this book and why you are reading it. Make no mistake—*we* are playing to win.

No one sits down for a chess game wanting to lose. No one wakes up with hopes of having a terrible day. No one goes to work wishing they never got promoted. I have officiated 43 weddings and I've never met a couple who hoped they'd get a divorce. Yes—you play to win the game!

"...you play to win the game. Hello? You don't just play to play it!"

Coach Herm Edwards

Checkmate is what wins the chess game. You have finally put your opponent's king in an inescapable position. Your rival's king is *checked* and has nowhere to safely move without being captured or *mated*. Congratulations, you won! The first time I uttered the words "checkmate", I felt empowered and accomplished. The victory is even more exhilarating when you have finally checkmated your vision!

In many ways, a *checkmated* vision is your emphatic response to centuries of racial discrimination and unfair treatment. It's the counter-culture to decades of intentionally perpetuated stereotypes. It's your exclamation mark at the end of a tearfully written sentence. Your declaration that, "Against all odds, even when the system was designed to exclude me—I still won!"

I literally mumble "Checkmate!" to myself, after I have defeated a system of inequity and or have beaten the odds. Every time I become my vision and achieve my goals, I imagine myself beating another opponent in chess. When I defeat my opponent in chess, I stand up, grin, look in their eyes, squint, and shake their hand. As if to say, "Yes! I understand the game and I'm not going anywhere!" I'm simply recreating what my *popo* taught me about dominoes. He said to me, "Doron, when you domino—slam it and shout *"Domino!"* **Note**: Don't scream checkmate in chess, it's considered poor etiquette.

> *"...you are doing this for your grandchildren. You are building a legacy, creating a generational culture of winners."*

When you win and become your vision, you should celebrate. Being strategic is hard work. It's intense. It's not easy to approach everything from a methodical perspective, running a constant risk analysis, and always checking your core values for decision alignment. Additionally, overseeing a Success Map can be exhausting. You deserve to celebrate when you win, so please take one full week off and enjoy the victory.

However, when the celebration is over, it's time to ensure your victory is not just a one-time thing. Remember, you are doing this for your grandchildren or nieces, nephews, or godchildren, etc. You are building a legacy, creating a generational culture of winners. You must have this mindset if you don't want your hard work squandered or wasted. This is where you must start using the strategic language of sustainability and succession.

Sustainability is when something is self-regenerating, so it won't be depleted or damaged. It is when something can be sustained, supported, upheld, or confirmed.[xlvii] This is where I had the most to learn about strategic planning. Primarily, because many of us are first, second, or third generation successes, first generation wealth, first generation PhD, first generation *whatever*. In other words, after you have blazed the trail, you must keep the trail open for your heirs. You keep that trail open by ensuring you clearly write exactly how you did what you did.

It is imperative you ensure your process can be followed by anyone. This is where an honest postgame evaluation with lessons learned, pros and cons, mistakes and victories, etc., must be clearly identified. This is also how you keep improving your chess game. Most online chess games give you an analysis on both your bad moves and your good moves. The analysis also shows you where you could have made a better move and how it affected the rest of the game. It's amazing how many people just hit the *rematch* button and never review the *analysis* button.

In the strategic planning process, the final analysis is an overall performance evaluation. This is what helps you avoid repeating the same mistakes. You accomplish this analysis after your project, or Success Map is complete—after you have become your vision for that particular area or sector of your life. This is not your monitoring or evaluating process you accomplish regularly to stay on track. This is a final performance evaluation of how you performed and what areas of the strategic plan were flawed.

"Ensure your 18-year-old granddaughter can take your plan and achieve greater success than you did..."

Therefore, the last chapter in your strategic plan should be the performance analysis with proposed solutions. This is what your children and their children will refer to when taking on the family business or trying to accomplish a similar feat. Ultimately, you need to make sure your success is sustainable. Ensure that your 18-year-old granddaughter can take your plan and achieve greater success than you did. Now, that's sustainability.

According to Webster (2019), "Succession is defined as the act or process of following in order. It is the act or process of one person's taking the place of another in the enjoyment of or liability for rights or duties or both."[xlviii] And finally, it is, "The act or process of a person's becoming beneficially entitled to a property or property interest of a deceased person."

This is where we African Americans tend to fall short. We don't leave our children work—we leave them to work. We tend to get *caught up* and forget about our own legacies while helping somebody else build theirs. We spend a lifetime building up another family name and their generational wealth at the expense of our own. Okay, here's a **TOP SECRET** success weapon: Learn from the experts, and then create your own company as a *side hustle*. When your side hustle pays you more than your main hustle—leave and expand your side hustle.

Everyone reading this book should have at least three additional streams of income under a company or corporation named after you or your family. This is the beginning of your generational wealth. It doesn't have to be major. It may be cutting or doing hair, detailing cars, or occasionally selling BBQ out of a trailer. Grab your kids, put on your family jerseys, develop a strategic plan, create a way for people to pay you, practice your family slogan, and go! You must start somewhere. "Do not despise **these** small beginnings, for the Lord rejoices to see the work begin…" (Zechariah 4:10, NLT).

You must also have somebody in mind who can take on your business after you die—so, mentor your children early in the process. Teach them how to run the business! Involve them in your decision-making. We have tried our best to treat our children like business partners when it comes to our family wealth. For example, Erika and I involved our children in every facet of our rental property business. Both children were given a house and asked to assist us in managing the property. When something needing paying, was broken, or a decision had to be made, they were involved.

Listen, your children don't have to do what you did, and they may even have different career goals. However, if you plan your business correctly, you can create whatever job description you want for them. Create an executive level or c-suite role for them, send them to school, and then ensure they grow into it. They will see their place in the family business and get their degree with a strategic end in mind. They are learning with a purpose—this is a game changer.

To help your children succeed, you must have regular conversations with them about things such as:

- Succession planning (who's up next)
- Sustainment planning (how to keep the business profitable)
- Trusts, estates, and wills
- Life insurance amounts and instructions
- Who not to trust. Who to fire. (family included)
- Who to trust. Who to keep. (family included)
- Where to bank. Where not to bank.
- Your list of thought-partners and private funders
- Nonprofit and endowment planning
- Maintaining a set of common family names (i.e. Dorian, Erika, Faye, Anthony, Diane, Elbert, Ray, Savannah, Omar, etc.)
  - I suggest only using common names of people who have made significant impact to the family name, business, or possessed a great trait that others in the family should follow.
  - "A good name is more desirable than great riches; favor is better than silver and gold" (Proverbs 22:1, KJV).

Here are a few other things you can do to encourage sustainability and succession:

- Write a book, or books, on your journey.

- Create and archive family videos and/or lectures from the elders of your family.

- Keep and write personal letters or journals.

- Hold annual business meetings at reunions (discuss the family business, succession, and sustainability planning).

- Keep a list of patents trademarks, intellectual property, copy rights, etc. (I recommend you keep this in a safe or a safe deposit box.)

It's Your Move

Answer the following:

1. T/F   When you win, you should celebrate. Being strategic is hard work. It's intense.

2. T/F   When something is sustainable it is regenerating. It won't be depleted or damaged.

3. T/F   In the strategic planning process, the final analysis is an overall performance evaluation. This is what helps you avoid repeating the same mistakes. You accomplish this analysis after your project, or Success Map is complete—after you have become your vision for that particular area or sector of your life.

4. T/F   The last chapter in your strategic plan should be the performance analysis with proposed solutions.

5. T/F   We tend to get *caught up* and forget about our own legacies while helping somebody else build theirs. We spend a lifetime building up another family name and their generational wealth at the expense of our own.

6. T/F   You must also have somebody in mind who can take on your business after you die—mentor your children early in the process. Teach them how to run the business!

Let's Play: Common Strategies

It's not the big move that wins chess games. It's not the big move that wins in life. It's the small insignificant decisions and choices that are generally the most impactful. As a result, every choice, every decision must be part of a larger strategic plan. Here are some general and common tips to help you develop a strategic foundation when playing this amazing, yet complex game:

1. Move with a purpose
2. Play the middle
    a. Control the center
3. Advance both center pawns
4. Develop all the pieces
5. Answer all threats
6. Look for double attacks
7. Castle early
8. Make a plan
9. Take initiative – do not wait for your opponent to attack you
10. Control open lines

11. Simplify when ahead—trade off pieces in order to get rid of all the threats and minimize danger from opponents.

12. Play for mate or checkmate

Chess tactics often decide the chess games of players of all levels. For that reason, one of the main chess strategy tips for beginners is to start getting to know tactical themes right from the start.[xlix] Additionally, to encourage and develop your strategic thinking and the strategic skill of others, I recommend you join a chess club. There may not be a chess club where you live. If this is the case, start one.

When choosing a hobby, most people join a club to get to know others who share their interests or to profit from a membership. Becoming a member of a chess club does the same. You will also find people, thought-partners, who share the same interests with you.

A membership in a chess club is one of the best chess strategy tips for beginners and has plenty of advantages. You can have fun together with new friends, share your ideas and thoughts, get tips from your fellows, gain playing experience, profit from weekly training and so much more.[l]

THE STRATEGIC PLAN: PUTTING IT ALL TOGETHER

In a study conducted by Harvard Business Review, 97 percent of the 10,000 senior executives surveyed chose strategy as the most critical leadership behavior to their organizations' future success. Expert chess players agree. They know chess is a game of strategy. In order to win, you must have a better game plan than your opponent.

Yet, none of us just wakes up with a flawless strategy or game plan. As a matter of fact, the great ones know that developing a good strategy takes time and practice. They also know that having one single strategy is not enough. In chess, you must adapt to each of your opponent's moves. Therefore, strategy is not just one plan of action, it is not singular—it is plural.

Think of *strategy* more like your suitcase. When you travel to another country, you are not exactly sure what the weather will be. As a result, you must pack several things *just in case*. Strategies are your *just in cases* folded neatly and tightly packed into your suitcase. Only after arriving at your destination will you realize what you really need. Then, as the weather changes, you have a fresh set of new strategies in your suitcase. Remember, when *packing*—use the Three-Move Principle™.

You might need long-sleeved strategies, short-sleeved strategies, black tie strategies, business casual strategies, and bathing suit strategies. You must pack for every occasion. You need a strategy for every area of your life. Building on our suitcase analogy, we can now delve into strategic planning.

A strategic plan is a selection or group of your strategies all put together. Therefore, think of the strategic plan as your outfit—the shoes, shirt, skirt, and jewelry combination all put together. Like an outfit, the strategic plan is based on where you are going. How do you pick out a good outfit? For me I ask myself:

- It is appropriate?
- Does it match?
- Is it clean?
- Does it look good?

These questions are similar to what you should ask about your strategic plan:

- It is appropriate? (Is it going to work—can I pull this off?)
- Does it match? (Does it align with my core values?)
- Is it clean? (Has it been reviewed by my mentor or thought-partner for problem stains?)
- Does it look good? (Can it be clearly communicated? Is it written and put in a presentable format?)

Whether you realize it or not, you already have the strategic thinking tools to answer the above questions. You are ready for this!

Strategic thinking and strategic planning result in your strategic plan. The strategic plan is the result of your brainstorming and research work. It is a formal document, or written process that maps out the *what, when, why, where, and how* you are going to do something.

Officially, strategic planning is a process of seeing your desired future and creating a plan to get there. Companies use this type of planning to determine their objectives, core values, goals, and solutions to their threats and weaknesses. Does this all sound familiar? It should—you are ready for this!

As mentioned earlier, companies primarily use the concept of strategic planning. However, this book is about you applying the strategic planning concept to both your *professional* and your *personal* life. By reading this book, you are developing the ability to achieve strategic planning expertise. Strategic planning is identifying your vision, purpose, and mission. It's about exercising intentionality in goal setting and achieving success.

A strategic plan is your guide to help track personal and career-related goals. It serves as a constant reminder to ensure your life goals are in alignment with the things that truly matter to you. In other words, a strategic plan can help you grow as person and as a professional.

It's Your Move

Here we are. It's time to apply all we have discussed. It's time to put it all together. If you have completed the end of chapter *"It's Your Move"* exercises, this will be easier for you. Whether you realize it or not, you already have everything you need to create and finalize your strategic plan. If you have not, you should go back and complete those exercises. You are going to need that information before you go any further.

More than just a strategic planning framework, you now have a social and generational cause for accomplishing this work. You are now empowered with:

- Equity awareness and our generation's call to action (Civil Rights 2.0).

- Knowledge of how the portrayal of African Americans has affected our psyche and the need to *unthink* what we have seen and heard about ourselves.

- The need for visionaries rather than dreamers.

- How to accomplish a SWOT and/or a SWOTlution™.

- The power of identifying your strengths and embracing your weaknesses.

- The strategic power of thought-partners and mentors.

- The importance of establishing a set of personal core values, a mission, and casting a vision for each area of your life.

- A foundational knowledge of strategic thinking and decision-making.

- The generational value of sustainability and succession.

- Why you must be disciplined if you want to achieve your goals and become your vision.

- The necessity of objective progress checks and honest feedback sessions.

CHAPTER SIXTEEN

THE STRATEGIC PLAN FORMAT

What goes in a strategic plan is completely up to you. In some cases, what goes in the plan will based on what you are trying to accomplish. However, every strategic plan must begin with a few personal questions. This is a period of both reflecting and assessing where you are in life. Ask yourself the following questions:

1. Where am I in my life right now? Why?

2. Am I satisfied? Is there more I can achieve?

3. What's my dream? Is it realistic at this stage in my life?

4. What are my roadblocks? What are my solutions to those roadblocks?

5. Do I have the courage to do something about it?

6. If yes, begin the strategic planning process.

After reflecting on these questions, you should begin the strategic planning process. I recommend you go back and review the previous chapters if you need a refresher.

Strategic Planning Checklist

- ☐ Review, revise, or develop your core values.
- ☐ Identify the dream and seek the appropriate mentor or coach.
- ☐ Work your dream into a S.M.A.R.T. Vision and a S.M.A.R.T. Mission.
- ☐ Check for alignment with your core values.
- ☐ Conduct your research.
- ☐ Gather the data.
- ☐ Categorize the data (education, experience, and certification).
- ☐ Conduct a SWOTlution™ based on the data.
- ☐ Determine steps, activities, and length of time based on the critical path.
- ☐ Create your Success Map and review it for errors.
  - o Does it pass the common sense test?
- ☐ With your mentor, establish an objective assessment plan and divide it into four phases.
- ☐ Reestablish your commitment to discipline.
- ☐ Put your plan into a shareable format (more on this later).
- ☐ Follow the plan—become the vision.

After you have done your strategic planning legwork, you can now format it. There are many strategic plan formats. Some are very formal while others are extremely informal. Here a few ways to put your work into a format or plan:

- Written on 3x5 index cards and taped to the wall
- Microsoft Word document in a book report style format

- Microsoft Word document in a checklist style format
- Microsoft Excel© table with numbered steps
- Written on a chalkboard or a white board
- Written on different colored sticky-notes on a wall
- Put in an app on a cell phone or a computer
- Make into a PowerPoint© presentation
- Shown using flowcharts and diagrams
- Handwritten in a journal
- And so on and so forth

As you can see, there is more than *one way* to create and formalize your strategic plan. However, there is a *wrong way* to create a plan—and that's to not create one at all. A strategic plan is something tangible you can see and you can share with your thought-partners. I recommend using the professional report style strategic plan. This will also help provide you with a template to develop your strategic plan into a business plan if needed.

This style of plan can be bound, stapled, printed in color, and placed in a nice presentation folder. More importantly, it can be handed over, mailed, faxed, or sent to potential investors and/or partners. You can't easily give someone an idea on a chalkboard, sticky notes, or index cards. Remember, ask for help if formatting or report creation is not your strength. **Note:** This is a great time to leverage the talent of your thought-partners.

A strategic plan is not in your head. A plan stuck in your head is not a plan—it's nothing, and it doesn't exist. Here's another secret weapon to success—banks, investors, and thought-partners don't fund ideas. They fund plans. What's yours?

It's Your Move

The following template is developed so it can grow as your vision grows. Obviously, you can choose whatever format works best for you. However, I have used this template and have had great success in both my personal and professional sectors. I have walked a plan like this into major retail chains and banks, and walked out with funding—it works.

Additionally, should something ever happen to me, then my wife, children, and their children have clear and legible plans of succession and sustainability. This plan is part of your estate plan (more on estate planning in another book).

This format is constructed using a very simple, essay style format. You can do a quick internet search and find an easy-to-use template and very easily plug in your data based on the outline below. **Note:** You can also gain access to pre-developed templates, articles, research, and other strategic planning documents by subscribing to www.strategybrother.com. See the template below. Each number represents a new page:

1. Cover Page (Be creative and professional with your cover page.)

- Family logo or crest
- Family name
- Pre-made template

2. Information Page

- First name, middle initial, and last name (or company name)
- Your signature block and title

- Your mentor's or thought-partner's signature block and title
- Contact information
- Date/version

3. Table of Contents

4. Your Core Values or Value Phrases

5. Vision and Mission

- Write your vision and your mission for this plan

6. Data Analysis

- Education
- Experience
- Certification

7. Strengths, Weaknesses, Opportunities, and Threats

- Clearly written out, including expanded solutions to your SWOTlution™. For example:
- **Strength**—I received a scholarship, so I don't have to work anymore. I have more time to commit to LSAT preparation.
  - ⇒ SWOTlution™: Manage my time well, maximize my free time by studying and planning (and minimizing TV time).
- **Weakness**—I don't feel comfortable with my LSAT knowledge.
  - ⇒ SWOTlution™: Enroll in next fall's LSAT preparation boot camp.
- **Opportunities**—The LSAT boot camp instructor sits on the admissions board at the local law school. LSAT is offered twice this year at my school.

- ⇒ SWOTlution™: Perform better than everyone else. Stand out for the instructor to notice. Do the most! Work hard during boot camp knowing you are going to discretely ask the instructor for a letter of recommendation or a good word.

- ⇒ SWOTlution™: Take/pass the LSAT the summer after I complete LSAT boot camp, and apply for law school with the intention to start class no later than two years from the date I complete LSAT boot camp.

- **Threats**—Other students who have been in pre-law. They are also traditional students with no children. I am an adult learner with a two-year old son.

  - ⇒ SWOTlution™: Take advantage of my maturity. I'm a mother—out work them. Join their study group to ensure I'm retaining and applying the LSAT body of knowledge equal to or greater than they are.

  - ⇒ SWOTlution™: Ensure I show gratitude to my mother for taking care of my son while I'm in boot camp.

7. **Success Map**

8. **Evaluation Plan**

    - ⇒ Notes

    - ⇒ Assessment

    - ⇒ Updates

    - ⇒ Revisions

9. **Sustainability Plan**

    - o Can someone else accomplish this vision?

- Can anybody in your family take this and accomplish the same thing?
- Lessons learned

10. **Succession Plan**
    - Who will oversee this vision when you are done?
    - Who is next in line to ensure the generational success?
    - List of thought-partners.
    - List of potential funders and lenders.

If you didn't already, now you see the research and development phase is the most important part of the strategic planning process. Actually, that's all strategic planning really is.

CHAPTER SEVENTEEN

MY FINAL MOVE

Congratulations, you are well on your way to becoming your vision! If you are a parent, teacher, community pillar, pastor, professor, business owner, mentor, coach, etc., grab the person you love and get started. Start them at chapter one and help them begin their strategic planning journey.

You spent time creating a strategic plan for your personal and professional success. Now make sure you use it to guide your path. Remember, the most successful organizations have a plan that they use to guide their paths. You now have a small glimpse of how major organizations and highly successful people create their paths—they do it strategically.

It's time for us to realize our strategic brilliance, our already present ability to navigate life's complexities. I'm not a chess grandmaster, and this book was not intended to make you great at chess. This book was intended to show you the similarities in the game of chess and in life. As a matter of fact, most chess hobbyists don't even know half the rules or strategies involved in chess. Trust me when I tell you, the chess game is extremely complex—it still baffles the world's greatest chess players.

Likewise, life can be baffling. All of our options, complexities, and challenges can be daunting. This is why this book was aimed at teaching you intentionality. It encourages you to do everything on purpose. It taught you that you must plan to be great and you must walk in the prophetic power of your vision.

Lastly, chess is a game *we* need to play, a game we need to teach our children and their children, too. It fills in the strategic thinking gaps left by standard educational methods. Chess teaches the brain to use both sides or hemispheres. It develops both our artistic and logical thinking. Both types of thinking are critical in the game of life, and needed to navigate our spiritual, personal, social, and our economic chessboards.

We have to be more strategic and history has proven this to be true. *We* as a people have not always received credit for our role in building the wealth and the success of this country. In many instances, we were simply not afforded the opportunity to receive any credit or any of the wealth.

> *"...you have to face the fact that the whole problem is really the blacks. The key is to devise a system that recognizes this while not appearing to."*

Resultantly, much of our focus was on self-centered people who, because of our color, tried and still try to stop us from achieving our goals. Now, however, I encourage you—don't waste time on those kinds of people. Rather, spend your effort on the *systems* those people left behind, and the systems they are currently creating. Be strategic, as this is a long game. In other words, focus on the total cost of the car, and not the monthly payment.

I opened this work with a quote from former U.S. president, Richard Nixon. He stated, "...you have to face the fact that the whole problem is really the blacks. The key is to devise a system that recognizes this while not appearing to."[li] I disagree with Richard. The problem is not the blacks. As a matter of fact, "blacks" have been very solution-centric since being brought to this country. We have done some amazing things considering the odds. Here is a short list of amazing, and often unknown African American "problems." I hope this helps you remember, "You is smart, you is kind, you is important."[lii]

- Richard Spikes (created the automatic gear shift)
- Benjamin Banneker (created America's first clock)
- Alexander Miles (created automatic elevator doors)
- John Pickering (created the first blimp to have an electric motor and directional controls)
- Dr. Charles Drew (invented the method of separating and storing plasma, allowing it to be dehydrated and banked for later use)
- Lloyd P. Ray (created the dustpan)
- Lewis Latimer (created the electric lamp)
- John Purdy (created the folding chair)
- Alice H. Parker (created the gas-heating furnace)
- Garret Morgan (created the gas mask and the traffic light)
- Thomas Jennings (created dry cleaning)
- Dr. George Grant (created the golf tee)
- Marie Van Brittan Brown (created the home security system)
- Alfred L. Cralle (created the ice cream scooper)
- Sarah Boone (created the ironing board)
- John Albert Burr (created the first rotary blade lawn mower)
- Joseph A. Smith (created the lawn sprinkler)
- Phillip Downing (created the mailbox)
- Thomas Elkins (created the modern toilet)
- Thomas W. Stewart (created the mop)
- Otis Boykin (created the pacemaker)

- John Lee Love (created the portable pencil sharpener)

- George Crum (created potato chips)

- Lonnie G. Johnson (created the super soaker toy)

- Frederick Jones (created temperature control or the thermostat)

- Dr. Shirley Jackson (created the touch-tone telephone, the portable fax machine, caller ID, call waiting, and the fiber-optic cable)

- Dr. Patricia Bath (received multiple patents related to cataract treatment. The technology she invented, including the laserphaco probe, is used around the world to painlessly treat cataracts.)

In other cases, African Americans were not allowed to apply for patents due to inequitable patent laws. An amazing article posted by the American Bar Association (Jackson-Johnson, 2019) states, "The patent system simply was not available at that time to enslaved people—they were not considered American citizens, and the rights and provisions of the Constitution did not extend to them. In addition, states enacted laws that prevented enslaved people from owning any kind of property, presumably including patents."[liii] To honor just a few of these pioneers, I encourage you to do a quick search of the following people:

- Esther Jones

- Nathan "nearest" Green

- Charles Richardson Patterson

- Chuck Berry

- Henry Boyd

- Ned the Slave and Oscar J.E. Stewart

- Benjamin Montgomery

- Jo Anderson

Mr. Nixon's quote may anger some people—not me. It doesn't anger me, because it helped me realize I wasn't imagining things. It helped affirm the systemic objections and bureaucratic whispers I've experienced on my road to success.

This single quote was a breath of fresh air, because there is no harder enemy to fight than the one you don't know, or the one you can't see. Inequity and racism are real, and they still exist today—maybe not in plantations and shackles, but in rules and policies. This quote, and others like it, should only fuel our fire. It should fuel us to sit down at the chessboard of life and start making strategic moves. What will be your opening? By the way, when I'm playing white, I always begin with my pawn (1.e4).

Speaking of the pawn, I intentionally used the pawn as the cover art for this book. Primarily, because the term pawn is often used negatively and I believe we need to be freed from the *pawn mindset*. You must refuse to be used or manipulated. Keep working hard to get to the eighth rank. You can't just waltz your way there. You must be strategic about it.

Remember, once a pawn gets to the eighth rank, it can become any piece it wants. The pawn can be promoted to a queen, bishop, rook, or a knight. I particularly love the fact that you can become any piece, except the king. There can only be one King in your arsenal—the King of Kings. Hallelujah! **Note:** For more information on the King of Kings, and how you can get to know Him, please see Romans 3:23, 6:23; Acts 4:12; 16:30-31; 2 Corinthians 5:21; Romans 10:9; John 5:24; Ephesians 2:8-9; and Matthew 28:16-20.

Lastly, I believe a key component to having a happy, satisfied, and fulfilled life is to accomplish the things that are most important to you. We should accomplish the visions we have been given—this is much easier to do with a strategic plan to guide your career and life success.[liv]

Consider these words, "Then the LORD told me: I will give you my message in the form of a vision. Write it clearly enough to be read at a glance. At the time I have decided, my words will come true. You can trust what I say about the future. It may take a long time, but keep on waiting—it will happen!" (Habakkuk 2:2-3, CEV). Yep, God is a strategic planner, too!

Success will become easy for you. It will become a way of life. Before you know it, you will have created a wining culture. Soon, losses will be a shock to you and winning will be expected. You planned it, you saw it, and you strategized it. Be strategic BLACK FOLK—I dare you...

APPENDIX

IT'S YOUR MOVE– ANSWER KEY

Chapter 1 - Introduction to Strategic Thinking

1. Think about, assess, view, create

4. set a goal, create a plan, follow the plan, measure progress, revise the plan as needed, achieve the goal

Chapter 2 - Why Write a Book for African Americans?

1. True

2. True

Chapter 3 - Inequality versus Inequity

1. True

2. Starting point

3. True

4. Strategy, entry points

5. It did not address state anti-literacy laws, the literacy tests, and poll taxes. While it granted African Americans citizen-

ship rights, it did not account for the equity issues at the state level.

Chapter 6 - Decision Making: The Three-Move Principle™

1. True
2. True
3. If I decide this, what will happen? Then, what will happen? Then, what will happen after that?

Chapter 7 - Identifying Strengths, Embracing Weaknesses

1. True
2. True
3. True
4. Self-awareness
5. True

Chapter 11 - Developing Your Success Map

1. Success Map
2. True
3. Critical Step

END NOTES

i. Haldeman, H. R. (Harry R.), 1926-1993. (1994). The Haldeman Diaries: Inside the Nixon White House. Santa Monica, CA:Sony Imagesoft.

ii. Bradford, R. (n.d.). Critical Thinking: 11 Critical Skills Needed. Retrieved from https://www.cssp.com/cd0808b/criticalstrategicthinkingskills

iii. Williams, C. (2019, August 6). 10 Unmistakable signs that you are a strategic thinker. Retrieved from https://www.forbes.com/sites/williamcraig/2019/08/06/10-signs-you-are-a-strategic-thinker

iv. The Chessboard (n.d.). Retrieved from https://www.thechessdrum.net/chessacademy/thechessboard.html

v. Norton, David P. "Strategy Execution, A Competency that Creates Competitive Advantage." Palladium Group Whitepaper (2007): 1-7.

vi. Hanks, A., Solomon, D., Weller, C. (2018, February 21). Systematic Inequality: How America's Structural Racism Helped Create the Black-White Wealth Gap. Retrieved from https://www.americanprogress.org/issues/race/reports/2018/02/21/447051/systematic-inequality/

vii. Holy Bible, Proverbs 13:22, King James Version

viii. History is Fun (n.d.). The Jamestown Chronicles: *Angela Brought to Virginia* 1619. Retrieved from https://www.historyisfun.org/sites/jamestown-chronicles/angela

ix. Ibid.

x. Ibid.

xi. Raphael, X. (2017, March 1). How to Read and Write Algebraic Chess Notation. Retrieved from https://blog.chesshouse.com/how-to-read-and-write-algebraic-chess-notation

xii. Equity defined (n.d.). Retrieved from http://edglossary.org/equity/

xiii. Race Matters Institute (n.d.). Racial Equality or Racial Equity? The

	Difference it Makes. Retrieved from http://racemattersinstitute.org/blog/Racial-Equality-Racial-EquityWhats-the-Difference-What-Difference-Does-It-Make
xiv.	U.S. Census Bureau
xv.	Kleifgen, D. (2016, July 30). San Antonio's School Inequity, Rooted in City's History of Segregation. Retrieved from https://therivardreport.com/san-antonios-school-inequity-rooted-citys-history-segregation/
xvi.	Phillips Erb, K. (2018, November 5). For Election Day: A History Of The Poll Tax In America. Retrieved from https://www.forbes.com/sites/kellyphillipserb/2018/11/05/just-before-the-elections-a-history-of-the-poll-tax-in-america
xvii.	Wholesale Chess (n.d.). Chess Pieces and How they Move. Retrieved from https://www.wholesalechess.com/pages/new-to-chess/pieces.html
xviii.	Punyanunt-Carter, N. (2008).The Perceived Realism of African American Portrayals on Television. Department of Communication Studies, Texas Tech University, Lubbock, Texas, USA. The Howard Journal of Communications, 19:241 257, 2008 Copyright© Taylor & Francis Group, LLC
xix.	Ibid.
xx.	Ibid.
xxi.	Parker, K. (2019). Personal interview.
xxii.	Ibid.
xxiii.	Ibid.
xxiv.	Ibid.
xxv.	Wislow, E. (2017, March 21). Why a Personal SWOT Analysis will Help Your Career Growth. Retrieved from https://www.careermetis.com/personal-swot-analysis-career-growth/
xxvi.	The Atlantic (2015, October 10). Black Workers Really Do Need to Be Twice as Good. Retrieved on from https://www.theatlantic.com/business/archive/2015/10/why-black-workers-really-do-need-to-be-twice-as-good

xxvii. The Guardian (2014, February 25). Interview with Prince: Black people don't get second chances. Retrieved on from https://www.theguardian.com/music/2014/feb/25/prince-black-people-dont-get-second-chances

xxviii. Ibid.

xxix. Business News Daily (2017). How to Do a Personal SWOT Analysis. Retrieved from https://www.businessnewsdaily.com/5543-personal-swot-analysis

xxx. Mindtools, (n.d.). Personal SWOT Analysis Making the Most of Your Talents and Opportunities. Retrieved from https://www.mindtools.com/pages/article/

xxxi. Ibid.

xxxii. Ibid.

xxxiii. Ibid

xxxiv. Wheeler, D. (n.d.). A Beginner's Garden of Chess Openings. Retrieved from https://dwheeler.com/chess-openings/

xxxv. Emms, J. (2009). Starting Out: The Sicilian, 2nd ed., p.5

xxxvi. Ibid

xxxvii. Reynolds, M. (n.d.). How to Spot Visual, Auditory, and Kinesthetic-Learning Executives. Retrieved from https://www.inc.com/molly-reynolds/how-to-spot-visual-auditory-and-kinesthetic-learni.html

xxxviii. Sgîrcea, R., Castellanos, R., (2018, November 29). 5 Steps to Chess Master Decision Making WGM. Article retrieved from https://thechessworld.com/articles/general-information/5-steps-to-chess-master-decision-making/

xxxix. Scimia, E. (2018, August 8). Special Chess Rules for Castling, Pawn Promotion, and En Passant. Retrieved from https://www.thesprucecrafts.com/castling-promotion-and-en-passant-611548

xl. Chess Academy, (2019, November 24) Check and Checkmate! Retrieved December 2, 2019 from https://www.thechessdrum.net

xli. "Laws of Chess". FIDE. Retrieved 2008-11-26.

xlii. Stewart, R. (2005). The chess organiser's handbook. 3rd ed, incorporating the FIDE Laws of Chess. Harding Simpole, Devon.

xliii. Hooper D. and Whyld K. (1992). The Oxford companion to chess. 2nd ed, Oxford.

xliv. Ibid

xlv. Pro Football. Edward's Take on Jets: Quitting is Never an Option." Interview with Judy Battista, October 31, 2012. Retrieved on December 2, 2019 from www.nytimes.com

xlvi. Sustainability (2019). In Dictionary.com. Retrieved from https://www.dictionary.com/browse/sustainability

xlvii. Succession (2019). In *Merriam-Webster dictionary online*.

xlviii. Retrieved from https://www.merriam-webster.com/dictionary/succession

xlix. Chess Strategy Tips for Beginners – The Definitive Guide (April 30, 2018). Retrieved from https://www.ichess.net/blog/chess-strategy-tips-for-beginners

l. Ibid

li. Ibid.

lii. Shrum, J. (2016, May 2). 30 Reasons to Thank a Black Person. Retrieved from https://cw33.com/2016/02/05/30-inventions-you-can-thank-a-black-person-for

liii. Jackson Johnson, S. (2019). The Colorblind Patent System and Black Inventors Retrieved from https://www.americanbar.org/groups/intellectual_property_law/publications/landslide/2018-19/march-april/colorblind-patent-system-black-inventors/

liv. Creating a Personal Strategic Plan for Personal and Professional Success (n.d.) Retrieved from https://www.right.com/wps/wcm/connect/right-us-en/home/thoughtwire/categories/career-work/creating-a-personal-strategic-plan-for-personal-and-professional-success

About the Author

Lt. Colonel Dorian R. Williams, Sr., now retired, is proudly the Air Force's first ever black man to receive a direct commission as an aerospace physiologist. Dorian has three master's degrees and earned his PhD by the age of 33. Dr. Williams is a man of faith and has pastored, planted, or overseen a host of dynamic and multicultural ministries in the U.S., Japan, Philippines, West Africa, Guam, and Italy.

Also, an entrepreneur and business accelerator, Dorian has launched successful nonprofits, businesses, and has partnered with civic leaders on multimillion dollar community development projects. Known as StrategyBrother™, "Coach D" has created a unique and trademarked methodology which has produced successful authors, corporate professionals, consultants, nonprofit ventures, and much more. Dorian has coached an amazing 503 winners over the last two decades.

Dorian enjoys writing and researching Biblical History, Ecclesiology, Strategic Development, Leadership, Nonprofit and Social Work, Diversity, Equity, Inclusion, and Adult Education.

In 1995, Dr. Williams married his best friend and high school sweetheart, Erika. Together they have two amazing children, Dorian Jr. and Drew.

For booking information, please visit:
www.StrategyBrother.com

www.ingramcontent.com/pod-product-compliance
Lightning Source LLC
LaVergne TN
LVHW011944070526
838202LV00054B/4785